LEARN

Sue Co

Also available from Continuum

Sue Cowley: *Getting the Buggers to Behave 2*

Sue Cowley: *Getting the Buggers to Write*

Sue Cowley: *Guerilla Guide to Teaching*

Janet Kay: *Teaching Assistant's Handbook*

Angela Thody, Barbara Gray and Derek Bowden: *The Teacher's Survival Guide*

Sue Cowley's Teaching Clinic

Sue Cowley

continuum
LONDON • NEW YORK

Continuum

The Tower Building
11 York Road
London SE1 7NX

15 East 26th Street
New York
NY 10010

www.continuumbooks.com

© Sue Cowley 2003

First published 2003
Reprinted 2004

British Library Cataloguing-in-Publication Data
A catalogue record for this book is available from the British Library.

ISBN: 0-8264-6633-8 (paperback)

Library of Congress Cataloging-in-Publication Data
A catalogue record for this book is available from the Library of Congress.

Typeset by BookEns Ltd, Royston, Herts.
Printed and bound in Great Britain by MPG Books Ltd, Bodmin, Cornwall

Contents

To Álvie
with all my love

Acknowledgements

With many thanks to Anthony Haynes, Alexandra Webster, and Christina Parkinson at Continuum for all their hard work on my behalf. Thanks also to my mum for her continued support, and, as always, to Tilak.

Introduction

Welcome to my Teaching Clinic. In this book you'll find answers to many of the perennial issues and problems that teachers face on a daily basis in their classrooms. The advice that I give is designed to be both practical and realistic. Above all, my advice reflects what it's really like to work as a teacher in today's schools. The book is set out as a series of questions, covering the different issues that worry teachers: from classroom management and controlling behaviour, to delivering the curriculum, dealing with paperwork and lots of other aspects of the job. For each question I provide an answer that gives some general tips and advice, as well as a series of different strategies to actually put into practice in your own classroom situation.

When you're first starting out in teaching, struggling to control your students or to deal with all the paperwork, it's very tempting to feel that you're alone. You might imagine that no-one else is having the same problems, that no-one else is going through what you're going through. Teaching is, after all, a very solitary profession. Although we might be standing in front of 30 (or more) students in the classroom, the teacher is often the only adult present. This isolation can lead to a feeling that things are only going wrong in *your* classroom, that you are somehow not capable of keeping control, or of teaching 'properly', while everyone else is achieving miracles. Of course this impression is completely untrue, but the perception increases the stress of the job and can also damage your confidence.

This book is designed to help you feel less alone, and to find answers to the problems that you are experiencing. It deals with some of the most common concerns of student and newly qualified teachers, as well as issues which worry us more experienced, 'old hands' in the profession. In teaching there is rarely just one way of solving a problem, and for each of the questions I suggest a range of different strategies that the teacher might try. The strategies and ideas that I give come from my own experiences in the classroom, and from what I have learnt from other teachers, rather than from a theoretical standpoint.

Of course any advice is only useful in so far as it suits the situation in which you find yourself. For this reason, I give a number of different tactics to try in solving each of the problems I discuss. These will allow you the flexibility to adapt the strategies for your own children, your own school, and of course your own way of working as a teacher. The problems that I answer at the Teaching Clinic are ones that I have experienced myself during my teaching career, and also ones that have been raised with me by many of the teachers who I've met and worked with during the training courses I run.

Teaching is a complex job, and there are no shortcuts to solving the difficulties that you face in the classroom, especially with the big behavioural issues. Although I wish I had a magic wand that I could wave, so that your students would behave for you and always work well, unfortunately I don't. (Anyway, teaching would be pretty boring, really, if we only ever taught 'Stepford' children, who always did what they were told.) In the long run, the challenge of solving your own classroom problems will help you become a much better teacher, able to look at your own practice in an informed and rational way. Here, at the Teaching Clinic, is where that process can begin.

Sue Cowley
www.suecowley.co.uk

1 The talkative class

Q. *I just can't get my students to settle down and be quiet, especially when I want to explain the work at the start of the lesson. They're really noisy when they come in the room, then they just sit and chat, completely ignoring me, while I struggle to get their attention. I spend ages asking them to shut up, then when they won't I either just give up and talk over them, or I lose my temper and begin to shout. I've tried everything I can think of, but nothing seems to work. Sometimes, I've just got the class quiet, and I'm ready to start the lesson, when one kid makes a joke, and the whole thing collapses. It really winds me up, and then I start getting angry. This just seems to make matters worse. What on earth can I do?*

A. I've started my clinic by answering this question, because it's the one that teachers ask me most often when I'm doing my training work in schools. Getting a class to be silent when you want to address them is probably the single most important thing that a teacher can do to gain control of the classroom situation, and also one of the most difficult. In fact there's no over-estimating how hard it can be, especially when you're working with 'challenging' (i.e. poorly behaved, ill disciplined or disaffected) children.

There are a number of different approaches that you can use in order to get silence from your classes. Much will depend on the age and type of children you teach, the type of school where you work, and the sort of teacher you are, or want to be. You will need to use your own professional judgement (and a process of trial and error) to find out which approach works best for you. You'll notice that this question receives a very long and detailed answer, and this reflects both the importance I place on attaining silence from my children, and also how complex this aim can actually be to achieve. Before I explain some different tactics that you could use to get silence from your class, I'd like to make some general points about this particular issue.

- *Stick to your expectation*: I would advise you to always, always aim for *total* silence from your children, rather than just a reasonably quiet class, no matter how hard it is (and yes, I *do* know how hard it can be). Every time you give up on the expectation of complete silence, things will only get harder the next time, and the time after that. It's a slippery slope – once you've started heading downwards, it really is tough to drag yourself back up again.

- *Think about the signals you're giving*: If you do wimp out on your expectation of total silence, consider the verbal and non-verbal signals that this gives your class. Even if it's only a couple of particularly naughty students at the back who are chatting while you talk, you are still effectively saying to them (and to the rest of the class): '*it's okay, talk over me, I don't really mind*'. And each time you give out this signal, you are making life harder for yourself in the future.

- *Set the tone right from the start*: In the question asked above, the teacher mentions that the children are really noisy as they enter the room. Ideally, you want your class to be in the correct frame of mind before they're allowed into your space. For instance, this might involve lining them up outside beforehand, so that they come into the classroom in the mood for work. See the tactics below for some more ideas about how to achieve this.

- *Get them silent AND get their attention*: As well as an expectation of total silence when you address your students, what you also want is for every child in the room to be focused on you and actually listening to what you say. Ensure that all your children are making eye contact with you, and keep your eyes moving around the room to maintain their attention. It is all too easy for students to appear to be listening, but, unless they are actually looking directly at you, you may well find that your instructions are going in one ear and out of the other.

- *Communicate total certainty*: The teacher who has a crystal-clear expectation of what he or she wants (i.e. total silence and complete attention), is far more likely to succeed. Your manner should communicate complete confidence that you will achieve this expectation, and surprise or even shock if your students do not comply. The more certain and confident you can appear, the better you will find your students respond.

- *Use statements, not questions*: The effective teacher *tells* the class what he or she wants (politely, of course), rather than *asking* them to do something. For instance, rather than asking the class '*Please could you be silent now so we can start work?*', try instead saying '*I want complete silence, please, so that we can start work*'. The difference is subtle but important in terms of the message you are sending. Give them no room for doubt – you know what you want and you know that you will get it.

- *Avoid verbal requests*: In fact, if at all possible, it is far better to gain silence without actually opening your mouth. This may sound like a paradox, but the powerful and effective teacher will be able to achieve silence through non-verbal signals. In time (and it is possible with many classes, I promise), you should be able to gain silence through standing still, and raising a single eyebrow. Being able to achieve non-verbal attention in this way is one of the most wonderful feelings that a teacher can have. See the tactics below for some ideas about how this can be done.

- *Mind your language*: The actual words you use in the classroom are crucial, although the variations may seem relatively small. Your aim is to let your students know exactly what you want from them, so be careful about the vocabulary that you employ. You do not want your students to be 'quiet', what you actually want is for them to be 'silent', so be specific and tell them this.

- *Be polite*: In the initial question, the teacher mentions using the phrase '*shut up*' with the class. Being rude to your students is, however, a big mistake. My advice would be that you should always talk to your children in the same way you would to any adult. No matter how tempting it is to respond to your students' rudeness with a dose of your own, you need to set a polite and consistent role model for them to follow if you hope to gain their respect and co-operation. If you act rudely towards them, then it should be no surprise if they do not do what you say, or if they react in a confrontational way.

- *Stay calm*: The teacher also mentions getting wound up by the students' behaviour. This is, of course, only natural. However, it is also a red rag to a bull for the children. Seeing their teacher getting angry and losing control will give them a reason to repeat the behaviour again. After all, if you put yourself in their shoes, it's probably quite amusing to wind teachers up, and get them to turn bright red and start shouting.

How then do you actually deal with the problem of the talkative class? You will find three different approaches below: which one you try will depend on a number of factors, including the age of the children you teach and how they are likely to react to the different strategies. Much will also depend on your individual qualities as a teacher and as a person. For instance, there is no point in using the first tactic with students who might become confrontational and aggressive, unless you are able to maintain a completely calm and icy cool exterior. Finally, the tactics you employ will depend a great deal on the type of school in which you teach and the overall ethos of the institution.

Tactic One: Tough as nails

This tactic requires a lot of work and long-term commitment from the teacher, because it asks you to develop and maintain a very specific teaching style. However, it can be highly effective once you have it up and running. I've divided the explanation of the tactic into three sections: preparation, implementation and maintenance. Your first step will be to prepare for instigating the approach, your second step actually getting it to work, and your final step keeping things on track once you have achieved the silence and attention you require. This approach offers a very useful way to start the school year, setting up your expectations right from the word go. Alternatively, with a class where you've not yet managed to get complete silence, you might try this method at the beginning of a new term.

The 'tough as nails' approach involves the teacher sticking completely and without question to the school behaviour policy (or to a 'policy' of your own, if your school does not actually have a behaviour strategy in place). Every tiny infringement of the rules is clamped down on immediately, in a hard, firm, but always calm, consistent and fair way. The same misbehaviour always results in the same response, whether this is a sanction or other strategy. If you are normally reasonably relaxed with your classes, you will need to adopt a complete change in persona in order to make this strategy work, but it is well worth the effort involved when you achieve the end result.

Step One: Preparation

- Acquaint yourself fully with the school behaviour policy. Know exactly what the school's expectations of the students are, and exactly what should happen if they break the rules. Find out, too, what rewards are available for you to use.

- If your school doesn't have a set behaviour policy, decide on a set of expectations, sanctions and rewards of your own. You could ask other members of staff for advice, or simply use your own ideas.

- Write up a large, clear and unambiguous class set of the rules, the sanctions and rewards from the behaviour policy. Pin this up on your classroom wall, where you can refer to it quickly and easily.

- Find a method of recording sanctions that you will use from this point onwards. For instance you might use an exercise book to record the name of the student, the behaviour encountered, the sanction given and when it has been served. Decide on exactly what will happen if a child fails to serve a sanction (e.g. a particular length of detention or a phone call home).

- If you are dealing with particularly difficult students, it is a very good idea to have a senior teacher or manager present the first time you introduce this new approach. Contact the appropriate person and let them know where and when you will need them. It is important that they are in place for the beginning of the lesson, so make it completely clear that you need this to happen.

- In the secondary school, if possible, pick a lesson just before a break time (morning, lunch or afternoon) for the first time you use this new strategy. This will aid you in your quest to gain silence, as you can use the sanction of an instant break-time detention to help you get the class's attention. In the primary school you will have more flexibility about using break-time detentions with your class.

- Prepare yourself mentally for the approach. The keys to this tactic working are an ability to remain completely calm, and a refusal to get drawn into meaningless interactions with your children. Know exactly what you are planning to do, and don't let emotions, such as defensiveness or indecision, interfere with your success.

Step Two: Implementation
- When the class arrives at your room, get them to line up, single file, outside the classroom. Do not get drawn into verbal interactions with them. A command such as '*I want everyone lined up, single file, in silence, please*', should hopefully be sufficient. Stand in front of your classroom door and wait for a line to form, with your arms folded, looking as mean as you can (or instead simply with a completely blank face). If you feel yourself becoming agitated or defensive, try to ride it out without interacting verbally with the students. Use

alternative signals, such as looking pointedly at your watch or pretending to note down names. Remember: appearing icily calm is the key.

- If possible (for instance at the start of the school year, or if a manager is present), get the students completely silent at this point, facing front. Explain to them that you are going to have a serious word with them once they are inside the room. Explain, too, that you want them to go to their seats quickly and silently, and sit with arms folded waiting for your next instruction. Tell them that they should not get any equipment out (e.g. pencil cases, exercise books), as this may distract them from what you are going to say. Explain that, once they are seated, you will wait for complete silence from everyone before you talk again. If it seems appropriate, you could offer a reward at this stage for the whole class, or for individual students who do exactly as you ask.

- If it is not possible to get complete silence at this point, wait until a reasonable line has formed, then allow the students into the room, one at a time. As each child passes you, repeat the phrase: '*Straight to your seat, sitting in complete silence, please.*' If any of the children seem overly excitable as they pass you, indicate that they should step out of the line and wait beside you. When the rest of the class are inside the room, repeat your command to these students and ensure that they are calm before allowing them inside. Keep the classroom door open while you do this, so that you can keep an eye on the children's behaviour inside the room.

- Once the children are all in the room, follow them inside. Stand waiting at the front of the room, without speaking, arms folded and face impassive. If the class does not fall silent, hold your emotions in check, and guard against becoming defensive. Wait a minute or so, completely calm, to see if they take the non-verbal hint.

- If this does not work, turn to the board and write up a warning, with words to the effect of: '*You've been asked for complete silence. I am now adding minutes to the end of the lesson for a break-time detention. When you are completely silent, we can begin.*' You could draw a circle in which to write up the minutes then stand looking pointedly at your watch. Allow a full minute to pass before writing the number '1' in the circle to indicate the length of the detention, then another full minute before rubbing it out and changing it to a '2'.

- At this point you may find yourself becoming agitated if the children are not responding. Although it is highly likely that they will do as you ask, if they do not keep yourself as unemotional as possible, and simply wait it out. Remember, the world is not going to end if they do not comply – but they are going to earn themselves a punishment! The key is not to panic and give in to the temptation to talk over them.

- If the class are still not silent, then call their bluff. Give them the message that you will wait as long as it takes by refusing to talk to them, but simply carrying on with the strategy. Continue standing with your eyes on your watch, adding minutes to the board as each full minute passes. Eventually they will give in and fall silent – I promise! In fact, as more and more time passes, you will probably notice a snowball effect, in which the more sensible or well-behaved members of the class start to tell their noisy counterparts to be quiet. Please note that under normal circumstances I would not recommend the use of whole class detentions, because it tends to be unfair on the well-behaved members of the class. However, there is no harm at all in using this sanction on occasions.

- Once you have total silence from the class, talk them through your expectations of behaviour, and what will happen to them if they don't do as you ask. Let them know too about the potential rewards for behaving as you wish, and make these rewards ones that they are keen to earn. If you are not employing the 'hard as nails' tactic at the start of the school year, then explain the changes that are going to be made from now on. These could include:

- Lining up in silence outside the room, single file, facing the front, before coming inside.
- An expectation of complete silence and attention whenever you talk (and indeed whenever anyone is talking in the classroom, including their classmates).
- Implementation of sanctions as per the school policy for any child who does not comply completely with what you require. (If you are using your own policy, this is a good time to explain your rules.)
- A follow-up for every sanction set, if it is not served.
- Written work to be done in complete silence. (Note: even if you don't feel this is necessary, it is in fact useful to impose this expectation for a while, to maintain a calm and ordered atmosphere in the room.)
- Standing behind seats in silence before leaving the lesson.

Step Three: Maintenance

- If this approach is to work, it is crucial that the teacher manages to stay completely calm when faced by a student who doesn't comply. Try to remain as impassive, calm and collected as is humanly possible, at all times. Apply the school behaviour policy or rules in an almost robot-like way to help you keep your cool. Point out to your children that you are simply applying the standards that the school expects, and that you have no real desire to punish them. If they choose to misbehave, then they must accept the consequences.

- One of the keys to this approach is the willingness to hold out if your students decide to call your bluff by continuing to talk while you wait for silence. Having the self-confidence to do this shows your students that you are truly 'tough as nails': nothing will be allowed to come between your expectation and its realization. Whatever happens, do not give in to the urge to start talking over them again – remember that this sends the wrong signals and will only confuse them.

- You absolutely *must* follow up on any sanctions (e.g. detentions or phone calls home) that you set. The children need to be 100 per cent sure that you are going to follow through, otherwise the punishments will not work. This is hard going and time-consuming at first, but eventually it will pay dividends.

- See 'When sanctions don't work' further on in the book for some more tips on using sanctions effectively.

- Don't forget that rewards have an important role as well. Offer your children the challenge of complying with your request for complete silence and full attention, and ensure that you reward them properly when they do achieve the target you have set.

Tactic Two: It's wacky but it works

With many classes, an injection of humour or theatricality provides a wonderful way of stunning (or even shocking) the children into paying attention. Students respond really well to humour from their teachers (I suspect that they don't expect us to do something as human as being funny!). They especially like the teacher who is not afraid to be laughed at, or to laugh at him or herself. Classrooms (and indeed schools) can be rather boring, sterile places, and a touch of something wild or unusual provides welcome relief, as well as being a very useful and effective behaviour management strategy. The ideas below require the teacher to adopt at least a measure of the drama queen (or king) in the classroom. You will also need to use the art of bluff to implement many of these ideas, pretending that you mean what you say, even when you don't.

- '*I just can't take it anymore!*': I love using this strategy, and I've found that it elicits a bemused mixture of amusement and sympathy from my students. If you find yourself standing in front of a class who simply won't be quiet, sit down and start to bang your head on the desk, moaning to yourself: '*Oh why won't they be quiet? All I want is for them to be silent so that I can explain the lesson. I just can't take it anymore!'* Pretending to sob into your hands adds a nice touch of pathos to this strategy. When I've used this technique, I find that the children are unsure whether or not I'm serious, and become touchingly concerned about my mental state. You will also find that they do tend to be surprised into falling silent, either because they are sympathetic to your plight, or so that they can find out exactly what is going on – has their teacher really lost the plot?

• *Exit, stage left*: The great thing about this strategy is that it turns the *status quo* (of the teacher being an authoritative presence inside the classroom) completely on its head. Again, this often surprises the children into behaving themselves. It also demonstrates that you have a good sense of humour. Stand at the front of your room, waiting for silence. After about thirty seconds, simply cry aloud: *'Right, that's it! They won't be silent. I've had enough. I'm off!.'* Then storm out, slamming the door behind you. Wait just outside the room, listening with the door slightly ajar to gauge the reaction. Often, you will hear a stunned silence, followed by children asking, *'Where's she gone? Is she coming back? Has she gone to get the head teacher? Has she lost her marbles?'*. After a few moments, you might poke your head around the door to ask *'Are you ready to be silent yet?'*. If the class continues talking, push the door almost shut and stay outside. Only go back inside once the students are sitting in more or less complete silence. (Note: for safety reasons, this technique should only be used where the classroom has a glass window from which you can observe the children. If in any doubt about your class's reaction or potential behaviour, please do not try it.)

• *The 'way out' lesson*: In my book on behaviour management, *Getting the Buggers to Behave*, I describe a lesson that another teacher once showed me, in which he began the work by eating from a can of dog food. Unusual activities or lessons will always gain your students' attention and can provide a very useful control technique, and a way of gaining complete silence and attention from a class. At first, you may be faced by a rather boisterous reaction, but if you wait it out, the students will (99 times out of 100), fall silent to hear what you are going to do or say next. You will also gain yourself a useful reputation as a teacher who is going to teach in an interesting or amusing way, and this will tend to be reflected in the positive behaviour you receive. Remember, children do talk about their teachers outside of the classroom – if you eat dog food in front of them, or employ some other similarly unusual lesson idea, I assure you that you will be the talk of the school.

- *Big Brother is watching you*: I once used this strategy when I had a class that I simply could not get silent or under control. It does require you to use the art of bluff, to be willing to act as though you mean exactly what you say, and preferably to have a sympathetic head teacher. Set up a video camera in the corner of the room, and as the class enter, start recording. At first you may receive lots of questions and comments: '*Why are you videoing us? You're not allowed to do that without our permission*' etc., etc. Wait for the children to fall silent, and then explain to the class that you are so concerned about their excessive talking, that the head teacher has agreed to watch a video of the class to see who the culprits are (it doesn't matter if this is untrue, so long as the children believe you). Again, the initial reaction may be energetic and perhaps disbelieving, but stick the bluff out and you are likely to find that the class falls silent for fear that you might just be telling the truth! If your head teacher is supportive, he or she might be willing to come into the classroom to support your story. Incidentally, you can tell the head that he or she doesn't actually have to watch the video for the technique to work.

- *Call for help*: Again, the art of bluff is required for this strategy to succeed. Take out your mobile phone, or ask to borrow one from a child, and then pretend to dial a number. Wait until it is 'answered', then have an imaginary conversation with the head teacher or other senior manager about your excessively talkative class, and how frustrating they are being. You might conclude by asking, '*Would you mind dropping by in a while to see whether the children have become silent for me yet?*'. Again, the children will probably decide not to take the risk that you are bluffing, just in case the head teacher does decide to come in.

Tactic Three: Positivity

A positive atmosphere in the classroom is instrumental in helping us develop good relationships with the children we teach. Being positive is about a whole range of things: the way that you behave and interact with your students, the way that you set and structure the work, the focus that you choose to take with the class as a whole, and so on. You can find a whole section on creating a positive atmosphere in your classroom in the section 'The negative classroom'. The ideas and strategies explained below give you just some ways of using 'positivity' to get that vital silence and attention from your class.

- *Avoiding negativity*: The tendency with a difficult class is for the teacher to get into a negative frame of mind even before the lesson begins. It is very easy to get yourself worked up by worrying about the likely misbehaviour that you're going to encounter and the difficulties that you are going to face in gaining silence. This negative outlook often becomes a self-fulfilling prophecy, because of the way it makes the teacher treat and react to the children, and consequently the impact it has on the children's mood and reactions. When applying the positivity tactic, take completely the opposite stance and refuse to give in to any negative feelings or reactions. Approach each lesson expecting the best, and try to react with surprise rather than annoyance if the children don't fulfil your expectation.

- *Right from the word go*: Right from the very first moment you see your class, be so overwhelmingly positive that they have very little choice but to go along with your (slightly mad and eccentric) mood. For instance, even if they are the proverbial class from hell, you might greet them at the door by saying,

'Wow! It's great to see you again, I'm really looking forward to all the wonderful work you're going to do today. I just know we're going to have a really fun time.' Once the children are inside, you could continue the positivity and get them silent by telling them, *'Right, let's see who wants to earn this fantastic reward for wonderful behaviour today . . . I just know you're all desperate to get on with the lesson, it's going to be soooo exciting. Let's see who's the best behaved child, sitting in silence, ready to earn the right to eat this Mars bar in front of the class.'*

- *Something to aim for*: Often, the majority of a class will fall silent, with only a few left talking while you wait. Then a child (aiming to be helpful) calls out *'be quiet'* and sets off a whole new series of conversations. Set a positive target for achieving silence as a good way to get the whole class working in tandem. For instance, you might wait until the noise level diminishes to almost nothing, then say, *'I want silence in five . . . four . . . three . . . two . . . one . . . zero'.* Something positive to aim for might also be a very concrete and visible reward, such as the Mars bar in the example above.

- *Praise one, encourage all*: In the majority of classrooms, the children's focus is at least partially (and hopefully wholly) on the teacher. This is one of the reasons why praising one child for doing what you want, rather than giving your attention to those who are misbehaving, can be so effective. Pick out a child (or a small group of children) who is sitting silently, waiting to listen to your instructions. Go to this child and praise him or her lavishly for such wonderful behaviour, perhaps mentioning all the wonderful rewards that the student will receive for doing as you wish. In many cases you will find that this praise of an individual is enough to encourage the whole class to fall silent, in the hope that they too will receive your praise and/or a reward.

- *Tell them what you want*: The teacher with a positive, assertive approach to managing children's behaviour is far more likely to be successful in getting what he or she wants from the class. Avoid making gentle and perhaps rather limp requests of your students, such as, 'Could you all be quiet now, please?'. Instead, tell them exactly what it is that you want by using a clear and firm statement. This might be, 'I want complete silence in 3 seconds, please', or, 'I want everyone silent, looking at me and making eye contact right now, please'.

If all else fails

In some situations, you will feel that you simply cannot get your class silent or even vaguely quiet, no matter what strategy you try. Although I would always urge you to aim for total silence whenever you can, I do accept that in some schools, or with some students, the struggle is an horrendously difficult one which may potentially lead to serious confrontations with your students, or simply might result in no work ever getting done. In fact one of the biggest frustrations of a talkative class is the feeling that you are wasting time that could be used on learning, and it is this that I believe often causes teachers to give in on the expectation of total silence. If you are having terrible trouble getting your children to be quiet, then the tactics below may provide some relief.

- *Divide and rule*: Even in the 'worst' schools, there will still be a majority of students who actually want to learn. As frustrating as it is for the teacher not to be able to gain silence, it must be a million times more so for the children who want to learn, but who are faced in many lessons by a class that is out of control. To use the divide and rule strategy, tell your class that those students who do want to listen and learn should move to the front of the room. Those who are not interested should sit at the back, where they may talk quietly. (You could warn them that you will be making a note of their names, and perhaps passing a list to a senior manager.) This strategy ensures that those who do want to learn can hear you, and you are able to get on with teaching them. Note: when I have had to resort to this tactic on occasions of complete desperation, I have found that the majority of the class does in fact move to the front, isolating their more troublesome peers at the back and creating a good partnership between the teacher and the well motivated students (usually, in fact, in the majority).

- *Plunge right in*: If you have a class that refuses to be silent while you're explaining the work, a good approach is to plan lessons that do not require any teacher explanation. For instance, you could have worksheets on each desk with instructions written clearly on them. You can then ask the children to start work immediately upon entering the room, so that those who are keen to learn can get on with the lesson straight away. When using this approach your role becomes more that of a facilitator than a teacher, moving around the room, dealing with any queries or incidents of misbehaviour while the children (especially the well motivated) are allowed to get on with their work.

- *Observe your colleagues*: Watching how other teachers at your school successfully get silence from their classes can be very helpful, especially when you are just starting out on your career, or just beginning work at a new school. This provides a very illuminating and helpful lesson in the type of strategies that are most useful at your own particular school, and with a specific set of students. While observing other teachers, try not to become disheartened if they are achieving a lot better behaviour than you. Do bear in mind that years of teaching experience and a previous reputation within a school have a very beneficial effect on behaviour. It might be a little while before you can hope to achieve the same results.

2 Off-task behaviour

Q. *I manage to set the work and get my class started on the activity, with everyone paying attention and apparently willing to try hard. The problem is, after about five minutes of working well, they start going off-task. It's nothing major, just chatting, doodling, the occasional child wandering around the room, and so on. I just don't feel that they're getting on with the work that I want them to do as well as they could. I've tried making them work in complete silence, but I find this almost impossible to achieve and, anyway, it seems a shame to have to be so strict. On the other hand, when I do say that they can chat quietly, they go off-task and I have to start shouting at them to get on with their work.*

A. Off-task behaviour is very irritating for the teacher. For a start, it means that your children are not achieving what they could and should do, and clearly this needs to be addressed. It also means that you must keep on their backs all the time, and it can sometimes feel like you are forever nagging at them to get on with their work. Do try to keep a perspective when you're dealing with off-task behaviour. Bear in mind that although your objective is obviously to get the best out of your class, not every child necessarily has a natural inclination to work hard all the time. Put yourself in your students' shoes and think back to times at school when you were bored, or when you had no particular interest in a subject, or when you simply couldn't be bothered to work hard.

Of course, as a professional, it is your duty to try to get the best that you can out of your children. In addition, you will have a far less stressful life if you can manage to keep your children on-task without excessive amounts of your own input. When you're faced with off-task behaviour, it's important for the teacher to consider why the behaviour is actually happening in the first place, in order to help you find ways to resolve the issue. What is the root cause behind the students going off-task, and how might this be addressed? Here are just a few suggestions as to what the problem could be.

- The children don't understand the task, perhaps because it's not been explained properly.

- The students don't know what to do because they weren't listening when the teacher explained the work.

- The task is too complicated, is poorly structured, or is simply not all that interesting.

- The work is ill-suited to the class's level of ability, being either too hard or too easy for some, or all, of the children.

- The students are unsure of just how much they must achieve during the lesson, and to what standard the work must be completed.

- The children are poorly motivated in their work, or (dare I say it?) simply lazy.

- The students lack the focus and concentration necessary to complete the activities that have been set.

- The work is boring, uninspiring or does not engage the class sufficiently.

- The subject or topic is one that the children don't particularly like or enjoy.

- The teacher is giving the class a negative mood or feeling about the work that must be done.

- External conditions, such as excessive heat, light or noise, are leading to a lack of energy and motivation.

Off-task behaviour will normally be caused by a combination of different factors within the classroom, probably including a few or more of those listed above. For instance, your children may indeed be very poorly motivated at school, but this lack of motivation could also be closely connected to the fact that they are not being offered sufficiently engaging lessons. Similarly, your students may not understand the task that has been set, not only because it is overly complicated, but also because they do not have the focus and self-discipline necessary to take in the teacher's instructions at the start of the lesson.

The tips below cover various ways that you can deal with the whole spectrum of potential reasons for off-task behaviour. I have given a number of pointers and ideas for you to try in various different parts of your lesson. These include the actual setting of the work, as well as considering the structure of the class, the students' learning needs and styles, and so on. See also the chapter entitled 'The little fidgets' for some more ideas about developing your students' concentration and focus.

Setting the work

Right from the start of the lesson, the teacher is setting up the possibility for, and expectation of, on-task (or indeed off-task) behaviour. Much of your class's working behaviour will depend on the way that you actually introduce and explain the work that is to be done. If you can get this element correct, you will be sowing the seeds for a successful lesson right from the word go. Here are some tips and ideas about how you might set up the work to create the climate for on-task behaviour.

- *Take an overview of your lesson's 'journey'*: When we set out on a long journey, it's important to have some idea of where we are going (and indeed why we are headed there). It's also crucial, especially on a long journey, that we are given the chance to take regular breaks to rest ourselves. View your lesson as a journey: at the start, give your children a clear idea of where they are headed, why they are going there, and how long and hard you expect them to work on the way. Let your children in on the secret of what the lesson will be about, and how it will be structured. Detailing the journey in this way is all about setting up your aims, or objectives, and sharing them with the class. Don't forget to factor in some breaks for your class, so that they can rest during the journey, and give them information about when these rest periods will be. Tell them, too, what they will be allowed or expected to do during their breaks. For instance, will you be giving them a five-minute chat time after 20 minutes' hard work, when they can talk among their friends about whatever they like? Alternatively, will you expect them to discuss the task during this time?

- *Make your explanations crystal clear.* When you are explaining the activities at the start of the lesson, do ensure that your children understand exactly what it is that they must do. I'm sure that you too have been faced by the situation where you explain the work and then, five minutes later, a scattering of hands go up with children saying, '*I don't understand what I'm meant to do*'. As you have planned the lesson (and because you're an adult), it is tempting to assume that your explanation of the work is clear enough and easily under-stood. This is not necessarily true, and it is important that the teacher takes time to describe each activity fully, and uses simple language in the process. As well as making the work itself crystal clear, do explain to your children the exact format or structure of the tasks you have set. For instance, how should they lay out their work, what should they do if they finish early, and so on?

- *Three instructions at a time*: It is very tempting to introduce a whole list of tasks at once at the start of class, especially when you have a great deal to get through in a single lesson. However, in my experience, I have found that children (and indeed adults) can rarely take in and retain more than three instructions at any one time. Aim to give a series of three instructions to your class and this will maximize the chances that they will retain the information. For more thoughts about this idea, see the section below on 'Structuring the work'.

- *Explain, repeat, explain*: If off-task behaviour is caused by a lack of understanding, you must take care to ensure that the class actually understand the activities set right at the start of your lesson. A good way to do this is to use the technique of 'explain, repeat, explain'. The technique works as follows:
  - *Explain*: First explain the work you wish the class to do in as clear and simple a way as possible.
  - *Repeat*: Next ask an individual child to repeat back to you his or her own understanding of the task set. You may be surprised at how widely this differs from what you actually meant.
  - *Explain*: After you've heard the student's interpretation of the activities, you have the chance to explain the work again, clarifying any misunderstandings.

- *Ensure you have their complete attention*: For the children to understand the work, it is vital that they listen in complete silence, and with their full attention, to the instructions you give at the start of the lesson. If some of your children are not focused on your explanation of the lesson, it is likely that at least some of their off-task behaviour actually consists of them asking their friends what they're supposed to be doing. For lots of ideas about how to gain the complete attention of your class, see Chapter 1, 'The talkative class' at the beginning of this book. I find it useful to insist that, as well as being silent and making eye contact with me, the children also sit very still. You can then identify any students who are fidgeting, as this probably means that they are not concentrating particularly well. With a class who have especially poor focus skills, it is a good idea to ensure that their desks are clear of books and equipment while you are talking through the work. In this way, there is nothing on the desks for them to play with and, consequently, no excuse for being distracted from the lesson explanation.

- *Worksheets or whiteboard*: It is always hard to retain a series of instructions in our heads and, for this reason, it is very useful for the teacher to write down a brief explanation of the tasks that must be completed. This might be done on a worksheet, or simply as a brief list of pointers on a class whiteboard or chalk board. The teacher can then refer to this list of tasks during the lesson time to keep the children on track. If your list of instructions is very long, it is worth dividing it up into the three instructions at a time, as discussed above. A useful idea is to get the class involved in writing the list of tasks, perhaps using this as a reward for those children who appear to be concentrating particularly well.

- *Make it sound exciting*: When you are introducing your lessons, try to do so in a positive and enthusiastic way. If your own mood and approach suggests that the work is exciting and interesting, you are far more likely to gain a good response from your children, and consequently to encourage on-task behaviour. I find that I can communicate a great deal of energy and excitement simply through the tone of my voice. Just as you might use a variety of different 'voices' to read a story (from loud to whispered, from happy to sad), so you can suggest how exciting a topic or task is simply through the way that you make it sound.

- *Give them a 'hook'*: I feel very strongly that we should make our lessons as interesting as possible, as often as we can. Obviously this is not possible all of the time, but the effective teacher will certainly aim to make the majority of the work engaging. You will find that this has a knock-on effect on the way that your class approaches activities, and on how well they stay on-task. If your children go off-task because they lack motivation, it is all the more vital that you find some way of hooking them into the work and of engaging their attention and their interest. There is a huge number of different hooks with which you might spark your children's imagination. For instance, your hook might be a prop connected to the topic you are studying, or a piece of music to set the atmosphere in the classroom. When considering what hook you could use, try putting yourself in your children's shoes to consider what teaching resources or approaches you would find engaging if you were a student being asked to do this particular lesson.

- *Set your sights high*: In my experience, children are more likely to get involved with the work you give them if you have high expectations of what they can achieve. Although you obviously need to ensure that the work is not too difficult for the children's ability levels, you should also try to find activities that do stretch them. This is particularly important for the most able students in your class. There is no harm at all in introducing advanced concepts and technical terms to your class. In fact being given this type of work can be very motivating for your students – they feel proud that their teacher has trusted them with such high-level work. For more ideas about examples about how you can achieve this, see the chapter on 'The class of widely varying abilities'.

Structuring the work

With the pressure to get through the curriculum, it is tempting to focus on lesson content and to lose sight of how important delivery is. When you are structuring a lesson for a class that tends to go off-task, you do need to think very carefully about the learning styles that will work best in motivating your students and keeping them on task. The tips below will help you in the process of structuring your work to achieve on-task behaviour.

- *Break the journey up*: In the previous section, I used the metaphor of a journey to describe the lesson. To keep the children focused on your journey (or lesson), a very useful tip is to break the work up into a series of short tasks. For children with poor concentration, it is difficult to stay focused on one piece of work for a long period of time. Setting a series of quick tasks (each perhaps taking 10 minutes), with a reward at the end (maybe a minute to chat with a partner), is an excellent way of avoiding off-task behaviour. By dividing up the work in this way, you also have the chance to regain the children's attention at various points throughout the lesson, to share and praise any examples of good work, and to explain the task that will follow.

- *Use a mixture of tasks*: I think that some teachers (including myself) are overly keen on the sound of their own voices. I love teaching, and the temptation to go on and on at my classes to explain a point about my subject in excessive detail, means that I can get channelled into doing a great deal of teacher-led work, which might not necessarily be the best approach for my children. We need to fight against this urge. When dealing with off-task behaviour, the sensible teacher looks at his or her teaching style from the children's perspective, and uses a wide mixture of different types of task, to retain the students' interest. This could include group work, paired work, drawing as well as writing, whole class debates, small group feedback to the class, and so on. Basically, anything that avoids long periods in which the children must listen to the teacher droning on!

- *Use 'time-outs'*: If your children have poor concentration, the offer of 'time-outs' during the class, in return for sustained periods of work, provides a very useful carrot to reward on-task behaviour. A short time spent deliberately off-task (or on an alternative activity) will be balanced by the quality of work put in during the rest of the lesson. Depending on the children you teach, you might allow the time-outs to be a chance for a quick chat with a friend, or alternatively you might focus the time-outs on discussion about the work.

- *Punctuate the lesson time*: In addition to the time-outs described above, there are other ways in which you can punctuate or break-up the lesson time. For instance, you might stop the class and get everyone to stand up and 'shake out' their bodies, or do some other form of quick physical or mental activity. These 'punctuations' give the children the opportunity to have a quick and preferably physically active break from class work that, in the majority of subjects, does tend to be fairly static. If you do happen to teach a more active area of the curriculum, such as music or PE, then your punctuations might be short activities designed to calm down and rest the class. For instance, asking the children to freeze as still as statues for a brief time, perhaps a couple of minutes.

Classroom management issues

In addition to looking at ways of setting and structuring the work to maximize on-task behaviour, there are also various classroom management issues that you should consider. The way that you manage the children will have a strong impact on the way that they approach the activities that you set. The ideas given below will help you organize your classroom effectively, and ensure that you keep your students on-task as much as possible.

- *Consider your grouping and seating arrangements*: If your children are not fulfilling your expectation of hard work and concentration, you are perfectly entitled to sanction them. One useful way to do this, and simultaneously to encourage better working behaviour, is by moving them around within the space. Draw up a seating plan, perhaps one in which girls sit next to boys if you believe this would be most effective. You can then offer the reward for on-task behaviour (over a sustained period) of allowing the children to return to seating positions of their own choice.

- *Be tough enough*: Although the teacher asking the question says it is 'a shame' to have to be strict, with some classes this is exactly what is required. It could be that you simply need to stamp down on your students for a while, to make them work in silence, or sanction them for a lack of application or effort. The teacher can always relax this expectation a little after a few weeks of really hard work, with the proviso that the strict approach will be reinstated if the children do not continue to work as well as you require.

- *Relax a bit*: On the other hand, do bear in mind that, as the saying goes, 'kids will be kids'. Very few of us (even as adults) really want to work hard all the time. It's tempting for the teacher to continually crack the whip in order to get through the curriculum, or for you to feel that your children must work to the absolute best of their ability at all times. However, this expectation is not necessarily realistic, nor is it always the best way to get the highest quality work out of your students. Do use the idea of time-outs or punctuations, as suggested above, to allow your children a break during the lesson, and consider starting the process of negotiation described below. Remember, too, not to be excessively perfectionist in your expectations of what your children will achieve. At all times, bear in mind that teaching is a balancing act between pushing for hard graft and knowing when to loosen the reins a little. As a professional, you will know when each approach is most appropriate with your own children.

- *A process of negotiation*: In my experience, children work best for a teacher who is willing to negotiate realistic, but tough, targets for the amount and quality of the work that must be done. They seem to sense when a teacher is being fair, at the same time as pushing them to achieve the best that they can. Discuss with your students the length of time you want them to work in one go, and how hard they should work during that period. Remember to listen to what they have to say on the subject, rather than simply imposing your own ideas. Offer them a break after a reasonable period of work as part of the negotiating process. That way you can develop a sense of partnership with your class – effectively you as their teacher are saying: '*I need you to work, and work hard (for your own sake), but I am fair and realistic and I do understand that you need breaks from time to time.*'

- *Using rewards*: The human inclination is to work harder, and with more focus, if there is a tangible reward on offer at the end. When we leave education and get a job, we receive a clear reward for the pain of having to get up early in the morning and work hard all day. For some, the most important carrot is the promise of a salary at the end of the week or month; for others, a large part of the reward is the satisfaction of doing a good job, perhaps fulfilling a vocation such as teaching or nursing. School is a rather artificial environment when it comes to rewarding hard work and high achievement. For some students, the motivation of doing well and achieving good results is enough; for others, the teacher needs to offer additional rewards to promote on-task behaviour. When you break up the journey of the lesson, as described above, you give yourself the opportunity to use a series of rewards during your lessons. Pounce on every opportunity that presents itself to reward your children for what they achieve during the course of your journey together, whether this is for good effort, for high quality of work, or simply for concentrating a little better than in the lesson before.

Student issues

Sometimes, the issues about going off-task will be to do with your students, rather than with your lesson delivery or your organizational skills as a teacher. You might be working with children who have never been taught the meaning of good working behaviour, or who have never learnt how to concentrate for any length of time. If this is the case in your school, there are still a number of ways in which you can have an impact on the situation. Many of the ideas discussed below are to do with the notion of training your children in what is meant by good working behaviour. For some students, this training is unnecessary, probably because they have received clear boundaries and good instruction in the home, before arriving at school. For many children, however, the strategies given below will prove of help, both now and in their future schooling.

- *Teach them what 'on-task' means*: It's very important to make it crystal clear to your students exactly what you do mean by 'on-task' behaviour. Unless they are certain about this, it is likely that they will push at the limits to see where your boundaries actually are and how serious you are about sticking to them. Give your children a totally clear outline of what you mean by being on-task. Talk them through your expectations, putting a list of work rules up on the classroom wall so that you can refer to them as necessary. Spend time explaining what sanctions will be used for those who refuse to comply with your expectation of hard work and on-task behaviour. Bear in mind that different teachers will have widely varying ideas of what working on-task means. For a child in the secondary school, this will be particularly confusing, as they move from class to class and experience a variety of different expectation levels. Your on-task behaviour might include working in silence, not getting out of their seats, completing a set amount of work and so on. Make all this clear to your children right from the start.

- *Teach them how to concentrate*: For some children, maintaining concentration for an extended period of time is actually very difficult, perhaps because this skill has not been developed in the home. There are a number of things that the teacher can do to help his or her students actually learn how to concentrate. Focus exercises are very useful in teaching concentration skills. For instance, one very simple example is asking your class to shut their eyes and focus on the sounds that they can hear, both inside and outside the classroom, for a few minutes. This helps your children to calm themselves and prepare for the work they are about to do. You can find lots more ideas for focus exercises in my book '*Getting the Buggers to Write*' (London: Continuum, 2002).

- *Use work guaranteed to engage them*: Consider whether the work that you are setting is the root cause of the issues with your students going off-task. Are they simply getting bored or frustrated by work that they see as too easy, not exciting enough, or alternatively by work that is too difficult or simply poorly explained? Think of ways to catch your students' attention at the beginning of the class. If the work is motivating, engaging and at the appropriate level, your children will tend to stick at it, and they will gain a positive sense of achievement when it is completed. If it is not, then this could be the reason for off-task behaviour.

- *Take time to differentiate*: It's always a complex task for the teacher to differentiate the work for the whole range of students, simply because there will be such a large number of children in your class or classes. However, you do need to accept that in many cases off-task behaviour is a result of a mismatch between the work and the children's learning needs. If your class does include children with a range of differing needs, then time and energy spent on differentiating the work will probably result in far less energy being spent on managing behaviour and in keeping the children on-task. The quality of the learning that takes place is likely to rise substantially as well. For lots of ideas about how to differentiate for students with different ability levels, see the chapter on 'The class of widely varying abilities'.

• *Celebrate good work*: When your class do produce good work, having stayed on-task during the lesson, do ensure that you celebrate this in a suitably lavish manner. It could be that you only reward a select group of students who have actually done as you wish. Rewarding achievement in this way will help encourage those who don't complete or stick at their work to try harder. Celebrating good work might mean giving merits or stickers, setting up displays, publishing writing in a school magazine or on the Internet, or simply reading out high quality pieces of work to the class.

3 The developing confrontation

Q. *Every time I have to tell a child off, or give out a sanction, the situation quickly descends into a slanging match between me and the student. I want the class to understand that I'm going to pick up on misbehaviour, but every time I tell someone off I get faced by defiance, or rudeness, or sometimes the student just completely ignores me. When this happens, I get really angry and wound up. I start shouting at the child in front of the whole class, even though I know that I shouldn't. Eventually, what started as a simple telling-off ends with the kid swearing at me, or storming out of the room, or both. These constant confrontations are starting to undermine my authority with the class as a whole, and I can feel my control starting to slip away. I also find them really stressful on a personal level, and often end up in tears in the staff room afterwards. I'm beginning to dread going into work and facing the children. What can I do to resolve this problem?*

A. As the teacher in the question has discovered, there is nothing simple or straightforward about disciplining children who misbehave. Human nature means that a child's natural reaction to being told off is inevitably one of defensiveness and hostility. It is only if the teacher uses a wide range of subtle skills and techniques that problems with confrontations can be avoided. Let's face it, none of us like to be reprimanded and there is no reason at all why this should be any easier for a child to take than for an adult. In fact, it is probably more difficult for the child, because the teacher is in a position of authority and consequently has more power and status. This can mean that your students experience a range of emotions and reactions when being told off by a teacher: from fear to defiance, from submission to anger.

Once a series of confrontations has taken place, the teacher might get into a defensive position, expecting problems to arise every time the class is taught. Of course, this defensiveness communicates itself to the students in the way that the teacher deals with them, worsening the situation and creating a great deal of stress for both parties. Ideally, the teacher should approach his or her class in a very positive manner every single time they meet, refusing to get drawn into negative encounters. (I am of course aware of how difficult this is with some classes!) You will find lots more ideas for developing and maintaining a positive approach with your children in the chapter on 'The negative classroom'. In the answer that follows I focus mainly on what happens once you do have to start disciplining or sanctioning a child, and how you can make the process run as smoothly as possible.

The tips, strategies and suggestions below give a whole range of different techniques that should be combined to make disciplining and sanctioning an effective and non-confrontational process. Which of these strategies you use will depend on the type of children in your class and the type of school at which you teach. The tips are offered in a series of stages: from the initial interaction, through the teacher's approach, looking at the student and the behaviour, and finally to the aftermath of the situation. After this, you will find a scenario in which the teacher puts into practice some of the strategies that I have suggested.

Stage One: The initial interaction

Very often, it is in the first few moments after an incident of misbehaviour that a potential conflict is either set into motion, or stopped in its tracks. The teacher controls much of what happens at this stage, and it is his or her reaction to the situation that will determine whether or not problems arise. The tips below will help you avoid getting into confrontations in the first place.

- *Don't perform to an audience*: As a teacher standing at the front of the classroom, with 30 or so faces staring up at you, it can feel a little as though you are on stage, performing to an audience. In the question above, the teacher mentions that he 'want[s] the whole class to understand ...' and also says that he 'start[s] shouting at the child in front of the whole class'. The problem with telling a child off in front of the rest of the class in this way is that your children effectively become an audience to the interaction. While this may in fact be your intention, you do need to consider very carefully what the tactic means in terms of increasing the likelihood of confrontations. In a situation where the class acts as an audience, both teacher and child have a lot to lose. The stakes are very high and consequently it becomes much more important to be seen to win (and of course crucial not to be seen to lose). If the teacher loses the confrontation, his or her status will immediately diminish in front of the class, and the same applies to the student who is being sanctioned. This factor can make the teacher and the student lose sight of reality and become far more defensive or aggressive than is really necessary, quickly getting drawn into the slanging match described in the question above.

- *Take it somewhere private*: Following on from this point, the solution is to discipline and sanction your children in private, as far as is humanly possible. If it is an appropriate point in the lesson, take a few moments to ensure that your class is engaged in the work. Then go and crouch down beside the child you need to discipline to discuss the behaviour in private. Alternatively, ask the student to step to the side or the back of the room (or even outside) for you to talk. This means that the pressure on both parties to win the encounter in front of an audience is alleviated. Any disciplining or sanctioning that is required can then be settled between the two of you, without raising the stakes by including the whole class as an audience.

- *Defer the discipline*: In my training work, teachers sometimes say to me, '... *but I can't get involved in a one-to-one discussion when I'm teaching the class, that's why I have to shout out across the room*'. My answer is that if you do find it is an inappropriate moment for a private conversation, then simply defer the disciplining until later. Make sure that you tell the child, '*I need to have a serious talk to you. When I've finished setting the work we're going to have words.*' This approach has the added advantage of letting the child stew on his or her behaviour (and its likely consequences) for a while, and also to turn down the heat a little if he or she is feeling particularly wound up. It also allows time for the teacher to step back from an initial emotional reaction to the misbehaviour (and this will often be an inappropriate level of irritation or anger), and to deal with the issue in a more considered way, when feelings are a little calmer.

- *Try to keep it positive*: Quite a substantial amount of the misbehaviour that we encounter is simply a form of attention seeking. When this is the case, it would probably be better for the teacher to simply overlook or ignore the inappropriate behaviour. Of course, if you do react by giving the child your attention, then you are actually reinforcing the poor behaviour that you had hoped to discourage. Naturally, if you are feeling defensive with a class, it is all too easy to over-react to examples of minor misbehaviour. A useful way to combat this temptation is to take a very optimistic and upbeat approach to the whole area of discipline (and indeed, to all the work you do within your school). Try at all times to keep an eye out for what's going on, in a positive way, in your classroom. Far better to praise the child who is doing what you want (sitting still, listening carefully), than to put the focus on a child who is not following your instructions.

Stage Two: The teacher's approach

As teachers, our main tool for keeping confrontation out of the classroom is our own approach to disciplining the children. There is so much potential in the way you handle an incident for either causing it to escalate, or alternatively keeping a lid on a potentially volatile situation. Always remember that it is not just the individual being disciplined who is watching and reacting to what you do. The class as a whole will also be making judgements about your effectiveness as a teacher by looking at the way that you deal with incidents of misbehaviour. The strategies that follow give you lots of ideas about how to keep things calm, and also ways for resolving the issue as quickly as possible.

- *Keep it quiet*: Generally speaking, the teacher is the focus of attention within the classroom (although sometimes you might not believe it!). If you tell a child off loudly, even if you are crouched beside them, then the class will tend to listen in to what you are saying. When they hear their teacher talking, their natural inclination is to pay attention to find out what you are saying. To help avoid this, either move the child away from the majority of the students in the room, or, alternatively, simply keep your voice very quiet indeed. Try to take a mental step back and listen to yourself for a moment as you talk, considering how loud you actually need to be for the child (who is right beside you) to hear. The answer is, probably not very loud at all.

- *Stay low key and defuse aggression*: The teacher can actually defuse a large number of potentially confrontational situations by taking a very low key, quiet and calm approach. Rather than responding to any signs of defiance from the child, throw the student off-track by refusing to get pulled into any arguments. For instance, in the scenario at the end of this section, the teacher asks '*Could I borrow your pen?*' when he wants to remove the source of the misbehaviour from the child. The child is far more likely to comply when the teacher responds in this way, rather than insisting that the child hand over the pen, and making a big issue out of it.

- *Stay calm*: The teacher in the question clearly has a problem with staying calm in confrontational situations. Of course, the natural reaction to a child who is being rude, or refusing to do what we say, is to get wound up, because we are, after all, only human beings. To avoid confrontations, though, it is vital that the teacher does not get angry. A teacher who becomes red faced and begins to shout is probably rather amusing and gratifying for the class. The children get a sense of power – '*We did that!*' – and consequently a very good reason to repeat the behaviour in the future, so that they can wind you up again. On the other hand, a calm, rational, even robot-like reaction to misbehaviour gives the children nothing to feed off, both at that point and when they are considering whether to misbehave in the future.

- *Use clear steps*: When faced by a rude or abusive child, it is tempting to dive in with the highest level of sanction (*'Right, you're in detention with me for an hour after class!'*) simply because we feel frustrated and probably angry. However, all this does is encourage confrontations because of the child's (rightful) sense that you are being unfair. When you have to apply sanctions, do so in clear steps, making apparent, at each point, exactly how and why the child has earned this particular punishment. This also gives you a useful carrot for pulling the child out of a spiral of poor behaviour. You can warn the child: *'If you continue to behave in that way, you will force me to apply the next level of sanction. Is that really what you want?'*

- *Don't threaten what you can't deliver*: The teacher who does jump in with the highest level of punishment will often be threatening a sanction that he or she simply cannot deliver. For instance, we are not allowed to keep children in detention for an hour after school, without first notifying their parents. Consequently, if you allow yourself to lose your temper, and threaten this as a potential punishment, you are in fact undermining your own authority. Eventually you will have to admit to the child that this sanction was in fact simply an empty threat that you have no way of actually enforcing. For lots more advice about using sanctions with your classes, see the chapter entitled 'When sanctions don't work'.

- *Put up a wall*: When we want to stay calm and avoid defensiveness, we need to avoid having an emotional reaction to misbehaviour. This also helps us deal with the situation rationally, retaining a sense of perspective and being fair to our children. When you are faced by misbehaviour, and you feel yourself getting wound up, try to place a metaphorical wall between yourself and what the child is doing. Let the poor behaviour deflect off the wall you have built, never allowing it to penetrate into your emotions. See the misbehaviour as the child's problem rather than yours – refuse to allow the behaviour to have any impact on you as a person and as a professional. You can find more thoughts on this approach in the chapter 'The over-emotional teacher'.

- *Feel pity rather than anger*: Carrying on from the point above, it is often the case that a child who persistently misbehaves does, in fact, have some deep-seated issues to resolve. It is likely that the confrontational child has learnt his or her behaviour through example, perhaps having been exposed to a lack of suitable boundaries or even aggression and abuse in the home. The appropriate adult and professional response to the child's problem is pity rather than anger. If you can hold onto feelings of sympathy rather than anger, you will keep the wall between you and the poor behaviour intact, and you will be able to respond in a calm and rational way to confrontational children.

- *Keep a perspective*: When you feel threatened by a child's misbehaviour, it is all too easy to lose perspective about how serious or important the issue or situation actually is in reality. This lack of perspective might lead to the teacher becoming overly defensive with the child, or perhaps sanctioning the student more quickly and severely than is necessary. When we are dealing with misbehaviour, we do need to understand and empathize with our children. Remember that some lessons will be boring and the temptation to misbehave will be high. Remember, too, that some children will constantly be testing the boundaries that you have set, unsure still of where the limits are. No matter how irritating it can be, misbehaviour is all part of a natural process of growing up, and learning what is and is not acceptable in our schools and in our society.

- *Don't get defensive*: When you are faced by confrontational behaviour, it is of course easy to fall into a defensive position, one in which you feel that the children are misbehaving deliberately, simply to wind you up or to get you angry. Most of the time, children are really not quite this conscious, devious or forward thinking about planning their actions. (Although they will certainly react naturally to a teacher who is easy to wind up, by seeing how often they can achieve this exciting result.) Try at all times to keep your emotional responses completely out of the equation, and to react as a professional, from a purely intellectual and rational perspective.

- *Lessen the threat*: Despite what we might sometimes feel, teachers do naturally have an aura of authority within the classroom, and a certain level of automatic status over their students. For a start, you are the adult and the person with the ability to punish them. In addition, the children we teach are usually smaller than we are, so we appear physically imposing to many of our students. When you are discussing a child's behaviour, or giving out a sanction, take care to lessen the perceived threat that you present. Children who are naturally inclined to become aggressive with adults, perhaps due to their previous experiences, are more likely to become confrontational if they see you as a threat. To lessen the threat you present, try using some of the following approaches:
  - *Get on their level*: An adult who towers over a child could give a sense of threat to a student who has experienced confrontations in the past, even if there is none actually implied. To avoid this, put yourself on the same physical level, or below, the child, by crouching down to talk to him or her.
  - *Keep your distance*: We all have a personal space and we feel uncomfortable if people come within this zone. Keep yourself at a reasonable distance from confrontational students to help decrease the sense of threat.
  - *Watch your tone*: When conversing with a child who tends to become aggressive, use a quiet, calm and moderate tone. Avoid talking 'at' the student and pushing yourself into the child's face. All of these actions can make the child feel threatened, and consequently lead to a confrontational reaction.

- *Never use sarcasm, or embarrass the child*: A teacher who uses sarcasm or embarrassment as a weapon against his or her children will inevitably cause more confrontations. I always recommend that teachers should treat their children in exactly the same way that you would treat other adults if you worked in an office or other non-school environment. Even when your students are rude, disrespectful or abusive towards you, try at all times to rise above them. Be aware that if you do resort to being sarcastic or embarrassing the child, especially in front of the whole class, this is asking for trouble and is very likely to encourage confrontations.

- *Be aware of your style*: The teacher in the question seems to be aiming for a fairly strict and authoritarian style with the children. The word 'defiance' in particular is one that is more often used by a teacher who believes in a strict and firm policy of discipline and order. Of course, there is no reason why teachers should not use this approach, but there should always be an awareness of the potential problems that it can lead to (especially for the less experienced teacher). As a strict and dictatorial teacher, your position in the hierarchy depends a great deal on scaring the children into doing what you say. It is consequently very easy to lose your status with a class when they decide to take you on, especially if you don't win every confrontation. This means that what should be minor issues can quickly build up into far more serious problems. It also means that the teacher might become defensive with the students when this is not actually necessary. There is also a greater likelihood of aggression and even violence arising.

- *Remember – it's not about win or lose*: Sometimes we get ourselves into a situation where we believe that we must either win or lose against a child who is misbehaving. For instance, you might ask a student to hand over a mobile phone that is being used against your wishes. If the child refuses, you then feel the need to win this particular battle by ensuring that you get the phone. Having a win or lose mentality prevents you from seeing that there are other possible options or strategies available, ones that are far less likely to lead to confrontations. In this instance, you might be better able to resolve the problem by asking the child to put the phone away, rather than insisting that it is handed over. Ensuring that you stay a step removed from your emotions will help you to keep the situation in perspective, and deal with it more rationally and calmly.

Stage Three: The student and the behaviour

If you do find yourself getting into regular confrontations with your children or your classes, one of the most valuable things you can do is to spend some time training them in the responses that you do want, rather than focusing on the behaviour that you don't require. What I mean by this is that you should help the children and the class learn how to consider and improve their own behaviour. Although this can be quite hard work in the short term, investing a bit of effort and energy will pay dividends over time. In addition to training your classes in how to behave, you also need to make it clear that your own responses to misbehaviour will be consistent and fair at all times. Here are some tips and suggestions about ways of encouraging your students to behave as you wish.

- *Get the child's focus before you sanction*: Sometimes, when we intervene with a child who is misbehaving, the student is not actually focusing on what we are saying as we try to discipline them. Consequently, the child might not actually hear or understand what is going on, and this can potentially lead to confrontations. Train your children to look at and listen to you when you are talking to them about how you want them to behave. Take the time to ensure that you have the child's focus before you even open your mouth. It is useful to be literally on the same level as the child, as that way you can ensure that he or she is looking directly at you. As we saw previously, this is also an excellent way to lessen the perceived threat that the teacher might present.

- *Give them a 'choice'*: When managing behaviour and trying to make a long-term impact, it is vital to put the ball in the child's court. It is the child's misbehaviour: the child performed the misdemeanour, the child 'owns' it (and is responsible for it) and you are simply dealing with the situation in which the child has put him or herself. Giving the student a choice can be very helpful, because it allows you to keep things depersonalized and very low key. When you are talking with a child about misbehaviour and its results and consequences, explain very clearly the choice that is available. For instance, you might say to the child who is refusing to do any work: '*You have a choice. The rules of our classroom require you to work. If you choose not to work, you will force me to apply the sanction. Is that what you really want?*' By explaining the two options in this way, the child should see the potential result of continuing with the behaviour and understand that it all comes down to a personal decision. The choice boils down, in the end, to two options: the student does as you/the rules require, or the child takes the consequences of the decision to disobey.

- *Take the children seriously*: Sometimes it is tempting for us to dismiss a child out of hand, to throw a sanction in the student's direction without making any attempt to explain what's going on. This might happen when we are busy or stressed, or when we have simply had enough of the children messing around. However, in the process of training your children in appropriate behaviour, it is always worth taking the time to explain why the behaviour is wrong, or to listen to the child's side of the story. For instance, if two students are arguing over the ownership of an item, you can show how fair and reasonable you are by hearing both sides of the story before coming to a judgement. It is also important to explain the sanctions that will result from the misbehaviour before you impose them. In this way you are far more likely to gain the child's respect and his or her compliance with your wishes. In addition, you cannot be accused of unfairness. In my experience, children do often feel that their teachers are being inconsistent, perhaps punishing one student more heavily than another. Again, preventing such a feeling will help you avoid confrontations.

• *Don't get sidetracked*: Often, when we're sanctioning a student, the child will attempt to side-track us away from the original offence, into a discussion intended to deflect attention from the misbehaviour. For instance, you might see Jimmy throwing a pen at Sammy. When you say to Jimmy, '*I just saw you throw that pen at Sammy, now I have to sanction you*', Jimmy tries to throw you off the scent (and proclaim his own innocence!) by telling you, '*But, miss/sir, Sammy threw a pen at me first*'. Stick to what you saw, and the results of this misbehaviour, rather than allowing the child to sidetrack you into a debate over what Sammy did. State what you actually witnessed and the results of that misbehaviour: '*I saw you throw the pen, Jimmy, the sanction you will receive is . . .*'. You're the teacher and you're in charge, so state the punishment that the child has chosen to receive (because of the misbehaviour). You can then move on with the lesson.

• *A two-way street*: Although it may take time, if you are consistent in applying sanctions for misbehaviour, eventually the children will start to respect you and to see that the decisions and actions you take are fair. Taking the effort to follow the strategies listed in this section will show the children that you are making every attempt to work with them in a fair and humanitarian way, rather than simply imposing your authority on them because you are the teacher. This sense of partnership will eventually stamp out all but the most difficult and complex of behavioural issues.

Stage Four: The aftermath

After an incident of confrontation has taken place, it is important for the teacher to understand and deal with any potential fallout. You might need to handle a student whose mood and attitude has been completely soured by a negative encounter; you will need to ensure that the child serves any sanctions that you have set; it is also essential to consider your own emotions and responses to confrontation, and to make sure that you take the time to reflect on and deal with what has happened. Here are some ideas about coping with the aftermath of confrontations in the classroom.

- *Understand the resentment*: A student who has been sanctioned may be in a bad mood for the remainder of the time during a lesson, or even for several lessons to come. It is important for us as teachers to realize that there may be resentment lingering and to take care not to exacerbate the situation. It is often sensible to take a hands-off approach to any child you have had to sanction, allowing them the space and time to settle down and accept what has happened. It is certainly never a good idea to rub in the fact of a child's misbehaviour or the punishment that has been earned, for instance with the use of sarcasm, no matter how tempting this may be.

- *Intellectualize the situation*: An intellectual, rather than emotional, approach to dealing with misbehaviour will allow the teacher to maintain the distance required to stay calm and rational. As well as reacting from the head (i.e. intellectually) during the telling off, the teacher should also intellectualize his or her own responses to what has occurred after the event. This will help you to deal with the inevitable stress that is caused by dealing with confrontational behaviour. Think about what happened rationally, trying to discover exactly what it was that caused the confrontation to arise. See 'Think the situation through', later in this list, for some more thoughts about the reasons why children become confrontational.

- *Give the child a chance to 'win-back'*: When a child has misbehaved, it is sometimes a good idea to give him or her the chance to win-back from the situation. This will help you avoid any resentment that the child may feel towards you when you give a sanction. For instance, you might offer the opportunity to shorten or even work off a detention during the rest of the class time. Rather than this being a sign of weakness, your students will in fact be very grateful, and will view you as reasonable and fair. I would, however, advise you to use the win-back technique quite sparingly, and only in circumstances where it seems particularly appropriate. This is because if you do always allow your children to win-back from their punishments, they may start to view your application of sanctions as inconsistent, and you as a soft touch. Perhaps you might use this technique when you feel that you need to build some bridges in the relationship between you and a certain student, or when a child has behaved in a way that is completely out of his or her normal character. There are various ways in which you can apply the win-back strategy. For instance, you might offer the child the chance to win-back detention time by working silently for the remainder of the lesson, or by completing a task of your choice. If a detention does have to be served, you could let the student shorten the length of the sanction by picking up litter from the classroom floor.

- *Use sanctions wisely*: Any sanction that you give will be far more effective if it is used for some constructive purpose, rather than simply being used as a punitive measure. In addition, if your children see that sanctions have some meaning beyond punishment, they are less likely to become confrontational when you do have to discipline them. For instance, if you give a detention you might spend some time while it is being served discussing the student's behaviour: why it happened, why it was wrong, the impact on the learning of the other children in the class, how the student might avoid making the same mistake in the future, and so on. I would always advise you to avoid using work as a sanction, because of the negative associations this creates – the last thing you want is for your children to view work as a punishment! Try to find a suitable 'community' activity instead, such as cleaning whiteboards, tidying cupboards or putting up displays. If the sanction you give is a phone call home, again this can be used constructively. During your talk with the child's parents, you could spend some time setting targets for improvement and advising the guardians about what they can do to support your work in school.

- *Think the situation through*: When a confrontation does occur, it is vital to consider exactly what it was that went wrong, and why the aggressive behaviour occurred. This is one of the best ways to avoid a repeat of the unwelcome behaviour in the future. There are many different reasons why a confrontation might arise in your classroom. Often a whole range of factors will have come into play to cause the situation to develop, rather than it being a case of one single thing that sparked off the problem. Some of these factors may be your 'fault', and consequently you will be able to alter your own teaching style or approach to avoid a repetition of the event. Others will have nothing at all to do with what or how you taught or controlled the class and will be harder to impact on or change. Below is a list of some of the issues that might have played a part in the problematic and confrontational behaviour. Once you have identified the problem(s), you can then consider how you might change things for the better in the future.
  - A problem in the home, that affected the child's mood or attitude when he/she arrived at school that day.
  - A school-based issue, such as an unexpected change in the timetable or a supply teacher taking a previous lesson.
  - Environmental factors, such as an overly hot or windy day, or a very high temperature in the classroom.
  - The child's mood on arriving at the lesson.
  - The child's attitude towards school as a whole.
  - A prior conflict between a group of children within the class.
  - In the secondary school, a conflict or confrontation in a previous class, or with another teacher that day.
  - The teacher's own attitude or mood towards the class during the lesson.
  - The content of the lesson – for instance a lesson that was too difficult or too dull.
  - The way the teacher dealt with a minor incident of misbehaviour, which then escalated out of control.
  - The use of sarcasm towards a child who was already feeling hurt that day.

- The teacher telling off a student in front of the whole class – giving the child a real 'dressing down'.

- *Look for support*: Confrontations can be hard to deal with, and you may find yourself feeling hurt and upset when a child has become abusive towards you. Do make sure that you turn to others for help: generally speaking you will find that your teaching colleagues and the other staff at your school know all too well how unhappy a confrontation can leave you feeling. The support you receive might take a number of different forms: it could be simply a shoulder to cry on, it might be another teacher advising you about how to handle a problematic child, it could be a senior manager having a serious word with the student and following up on the incident. Whatever form the support takes, don't view it as a comment on the quality of your teaching – see it instead as a much needed and welcome helping hand.

Putting it into practice

Having given you a whole range of different strategies to try out, let's take a look at how you can go about putting into practice how to avoid or deal with confrontations in your own classroom. Obviously, much will depend on your individual situation – the sort of school you work at, the type of children you teach, your own personal teaching style and so on. However, the advice below offers you a generic example to follow, and you can adapt this to suit your own circumstances. The following is an example of how a teacher might reprimand the children, and apply sanctions, in a calm, confident and non-confrontational way.

- The child misbehaves.

- The teacher focuses the rest of the class on the task in hand, or sets a quick activity for them to do.

- Alternatively, if the teacher is right in the middle of something (e.g. explaining the lesson), he or she notes out loud that the misbehaviour has been seen and tells the child that it will be dealt with in a moment.

- The teacher goes to crouch beside the child who has misbehaved, or asks the child to come to the side or back of the room.

- The teacher ensures that he/she has the child's full attention, getting proper eye contact with the student.

- The teacher either (a) outlines the misbehaviour as he or she perceives it; or (b) asks the child to explain the misbehaviour that has occurred. If appropriate, the teacher questions the student about the reasons behind the behaviour.

- The teacher gives the child a 'choice': cease the inappropriate behaviour now, or incur the relevant sanction. The sanction is described clearly, calmly and without emotion. It is a straightforward decision – stop the behaviour or this will be your punishment.

- If the child protests, the teacher refuses to get sidetracked. The teacher simply repeats the description of the behaviour, and the sanction that will be earned if it continues.

- If the behaviour does continue, or if it is serious enough to earn an instant sanction, the teacher explains how and why the sanction has been earned.

- The teacher talks about how the child can avoid getting into worse trouble, or how he or she might 'win-back' from the sanction in some way.

- At this point the child might try to sidetrack the teacher by complaining that 'It's not fair, it wasn't me who started it'.

- The teacher explains that the sanction is for the specific incident of misbehaviour that he or she observed, and that the child can either accept the punishment as it is (and try to 'win-back' from it), or move up to another level of sanction.

- Either: (a) the child accepts the sanction with good grace, and does not misbehave again; or (b) the child continues to behave inappropriately, and the teacher works through the process again.

Now let's have a look at how the process might take place in reality, running the steps as a scene from a typical classroom.

Ben is annoying Tommy, the boy sitting next to him, by trying to scribble on his work.

Tommy: *[calling out]* Sir! Make Ben stop doing that! He's scribbling all over my work.
Teacher: *[Moving over to where Tommy and Ben are seated as he speaks to the class.]* Right, everyone, excellent work so far, you've got three minutes to complete those questions. If you think you've finished, check your work carefully for any mistakes. I'm looking for the best pieces of work so that I can give out some merit marks.

The teacher waits until the class have settled back to work, then crouches down beside Ben and coughs lightly to get his attention. The teacher then starts to talk quietly to Ben, keeping a calm and soft tone in his voice.

Teacher: Ben?
Ben: Yes, sir. *[Ben is looking towards Tommy.]*
Teacher: Could I borrow your pen for a moment, please? *[Ben looks around and hands the pen over without thinking. The teacher has simultaneously got his attention and also removed the object that is facilitating the misbehaviour in a very low-key way.]*
Teacher: Thank you very much. Now Ben, I want you to look at me, please, so we can have a chat. Make eye contact with me, please.
Ben: *[now making full eye contact with the teacher]* What, sir?
Teacher: Do you know why I've had to come over and talk to you?
Ben: No, sir.
Tommy: 'Cos you was scribbling on my work, Ben.

Ben: No I wasn't!

Teacher: Tommy, I'd like to see how quickly you can finish those questions, please. You've got just a couple of minutes left. You might even win a merit mark if your work is really good. *[Tommy gets on with his work. The teacher does not want him interfering in their discussion and stirring things up, so he has offered a reward to keep Tommy occupied.]*

Ben: Sir, it's not fair, I didn't do anything to him!

Teacher: Ben, look at me please and listen carefully. You have a choice: you can get on with your own work and stop scribbling on Tommy's paper, or you can stay after class for five minutes to help me tidy up.

Ben: That's not fair, sir, I wasn't doing anything! And anyway, it was Tommy wot started it.

Teacher: Ben, I saw you scribbling on Tommy's work, so the choice is yours. Do as I ask and you won't have to stay behind, will you? You've got one minute left, let's see if you can finish that last question before the time's up.

At this point, hopefully, Ben will comply with the teacher's request. If he does not, the teacher can then employ the sanction that he has already specified, using the time after class to chat with Ben about his behaviour. Another good option to use would be to move Ben away from Tommy for the remainder of the lesson, as this would prevent the misbehaviour reoccuring.

4 The 'natural' teacher

Q. *What is it about some teachers? I'm an NQT, and the kids run rings around me, but there are one or two teachers at my school who seem to have a magic touch, who are simply 'naturals' at the job. It's not fair! There's this one teacher who can just walk into a room and the children will fall silent. This teacher has the students eating from the palm of her hand, they are just completely engrossed in the lesson. I walk into the classroom and the kids ignore me – they just carry on with their conversations and even when I start shouting at them, they don't do what I say. It's driving me mad, and I'm starting to worry that I'm just no good as a teacher. How can I get the 'magic touch' too?*

A. When we first start out in teaching, it can seem as though our colleagues do indeed have some kind of magic touch with their students, while we have to struggle through lesson after lesson of poor work or misbehaviour. Becoming an effective teacher is a very subtle and complex process, one which is never truly completed. As NQTs, or in the early years of our career, we still have a long, long way to go to become as good a teacher as we can be. The ideas and thoughts given below will help you understand exactly how and why these colleagues of yours have the 'magic touch'. The strategies that I suggest will help you gain that same magic touch too, although it will still take a lot of time and a great deal of effort. In teaching, there are no instant solutions to getting the kids to work and behave brilliantly for you, but of course this is all part of the fun and the challenge of the job. If it was easy, and anyone could do it, then it would be a far less interesting and inspiring profession.

I have no doubt at all that there are some people who are, what we might call, 'natural' teachers: people who are naturally good at managing children's learning and behaviour, and in inspiring their interest and attention. However, I also believe that a great deal of teaching ability is to do with learning a range of techniques and strategies to help you develop as a teacher. This is a large part of the reason why experienced teachers are generally better at controlling and working with their children than their inexperienced counterparts. Over the years we all pick up a range of strategies, whether this is through advice from other teachers and books such as this one, or simply through learning what does and doesn't work in our own classrooms. Although I would describe myself as a fairly natural manager of children, I certainly spent my first few years in teaching struggling, and making lots of mistakes, just as practically everyone else does. I've also had trouble when starting work at a new school, and having to get to know new and different children, and work with new rules, policies and approaches.

No matter how hard you find it at first, with time and perseverance, you can and will become an effective teacher. So, whatever happens, do try not to get too depressed or to lose confidence in yourself. I promise that it will happen for you soon, and probably earlier than you expect. Making mistakes, and learning from them, is all part of the process of becoming a teacher. Do be willing to experiment with different strategies and perhaps with some more unusual techniques as you learn from day to day in your own classroom. The answer that follows will give you some ideas about where to start the process of becoming a natural at the job.

Where does the 'magic touch' come from?

There are a whole range of factors involved for those teachers who do have the magic touch with their children. How much each factor plays a part will depend on the individual teacher concerned, as well as the children that you teach and the school in which you work. It may give you some comfort to consider the way in which the following aspects play a part in a teacher getting good work and behaviour from a class. Do bear in mind that, with time, these factors will be open to you too.

- *Time served*: If teachers work at a school for a long time, they will automatically receive a certain amount of respect and status. Sometimes it will be the case that a teacher who has worked at a school for many years is actually teaching the children (and even grandchildren) of his or her original students! In these cases, a kind of pre-conditioning comes into play, in which the children respect the years of previous experience. Teachers with a long period of service at one school will also have an advantage over their less experienced colleagues, in that they know exactly how the systems work, who to turn to with any problems, and so on. This certainty about the way that the school is run seems to communicate itself to the children, and they view the teacher in a different, more respectful, way, making the teacher appear to be a natural.

- *Management position*: It goes without saying that the majority of students will behave far better for a head of department, deputy head or head teacher, than for 'normal' classroom teachers. And at least a good part of this is to do with a healthy fear of what might happen if they do not! A head teacher who threatens to phone a child's home will naturally gain a fair amount of instant obedience, whereas a classroom teacher who uses the same sanction will not have quite the same impact.

- *Reputation*: Teachers who've worked at a school for some time, and who are effective classroom practitioners, will carry a ready-made reputation with them in their jobs. Children do talk about their teachers outside of the classroom (just as we talk or moan about our children in the staff room). Some of their conversation will be based around their thoughts on how 'lucky' or 'unlucky' they are to have certain teachers. The reputation that a teacher has might be one for providing fun lessons, or it could be for being so strict that students had better not misbehave. (Of course, reputations also offer the potential to cause trouble, if the students are not praising your effectiveness, but complaining about you or questioning your ability.)

- *Gender*: In some schools, and with some children, the gender of the teacher will play an important part in the way that he or she is viewed, and how much automatic respect is given. Sad to say, in our supposedly gender neutral times, some children do still come with (misplaced) preconceptions about how female teachers are 'easier' and less strict than their male counterparts. Happily, they are often surprised to find out exactly how far they are mistaken! In my training work, when I question teachers about who is a 'strict and scary' practitioner (see my book, *Getting the Buggers to Behave*, for an explanation of this approach), it is gratifying to see as many female as male hands go up in the air in recognition of exactly what I mean.

- *Teaching style*: The teacher who appears to have a magic touch is, of course, almost bound to be an effective classroom practitioner. He or she will probably have a teaching style that includes some or all of the following: confidence, consistency, mutual respect for and from the students, high quality and engaging lesson content, high level expectations, inspiration and enthusiasm. All of these qualities are available to any teacher (with, of course, a great deal of time and effort required in achieving them).

- *The true natural*: As I said in the introduction to this section, there are some people who apparently are just naturals at being a teacher. The likelihood is that such teachers are, in fact, employing some or all the strategies listed below without really thinking about it. If you'd like to become a natural too, you'll need to utilize these techniques yourself, so that you too can become a teacher with the magic touch.

How can I get the 'magic touch'?

There is certainly no easy way to achieve the magic touch – getting it takes time, effort and dedication. There are, of course, some strategies that you can use to help you along the way and it is these ideas that I explore below. Using these tips and techniques is all part of developing your professional practice and becoming the best teacher that you can be. If you're new to the profession, you may find some ideas here that you've not considered before. Even if you're an experienced classroom practitioner, with years in the job, you should still be able to use the strategies given below to refresh and develop yourself as a teacher.

- *Your attitude*: It is difficult to overestimate how important a teacher's attitude is in the reaction he or she receives from the class. If you can give across an air of complete certainty, confidence and unwavering belief in yourself and what you require from the class, this will quickly communicate itself to the children. This, of course, is one of the main reasons why the experienced teacher tends to manage behaviour and work better than his or her less experienced counterparts. To a large extent, the key to having an air of confidence and a complete certainty in your expectations is based on the lessons learnt in the past. As the years pass, you learn from the mistakes you have made and consequently you come across as a teacher who knows exactly what he or she wants. As well as displaying a confident and certain attitude about what will happen in your classroom, you should also try to give a positive, enthusiastic and even excited sense about the work that you and the children will be doing together.

- *Pace and energy*: A good lesson is like a gripping television programme or an exciting book – it has a sense of pace that grabs us right from the start. The natural teacher is able to communicate this feeling of energy – the sense of an imperative to learn. The children become caught up in the forward momentum of the lesson, pulled along on the tide of energy and enthusiasm generated by the teacher. Of course, it is not possible to create this feeling all the time, but the natural teacher has an enthusiasm which shines through, even in the dullest of subject or topic areas.

- *Love for the job*: Our students are very perceptive, and they are able to differentiate between a teacher who is simply marking time, doing the work but not really enjoying it, and the teacher who has a love for the job, and for the subject or subjects being taught. The children should hopefully get the feeling that you love your role and your subject so much, that you feel a strong urge to pass on this passion to others, and to inspire them to feel the same way. I can certainly remember teachers who gave this impression from my own schooling, and the subjects that they taught are the ones I have made my career from.

- *Expectations*: For the natural teacher, the expectation is that absolutely nothing will come between the children and the learning – between his or her students and the best that they can possibly achieve. Poor behaviour is discouraged because it is seen as a barrier to effective learning; lack of motivation is unacceptable because it means that the work is not being properly completed. The higher your expectations are, the better your children will respond to you and what you ask them to do. Setting and maintaining high expectations takes a great deal of time and effort, particularly at the beginning of your time with a class, but it is well worth the energy involved. Knowing what your expectations are is all part of the learning process of becoming a teacher, and as you gain in experience you will find that you do indeed know exactly what you expect your children to do.

- *Refuse to give up*: The teacher with a magic touch develops very strong and solid relationships with all of his or her children. This is particularly difficult to do with those students who are abusive or confrontational, but this teacher simply refuses to give up, even on these children. No matter how disagreeable the child tries to be, the teacher is simply unable to accept that the student might not be as important, special and capable as every other child. The teacher's attitude is that everyone will succeed – that the teacher owes it to the class to ensure this and that the children owe it to themselves not to interfere with their own success. For children who are used to adults giving up on them when they misbehave, or not believing in or celebrating their talents, this trust and belief is a vital part of creating a strong and lasting bond.

- *Get stuck in*: With a class whose behaviour is proving difficult, it is tempting to spend long periods of time at the beginning of each lesson moaning at the children and going over and over the rules that must be followed. Sometimes, however, this approach just leads to more trouble as the children get bored with listening to you complain. In fact, it can actually pay to just get stuck into some work right at the start of the class, and I have seen a number of natural teachers do just this. If the work itself is engaging and exciting (see below), then the issue of behaviour will usually fade into insignificance. The moment your unruly children arrive at the lesson, throw them straight in at the deep end with the work so that there is no opportunity for misbehaviour. It is a good idea to set the activities on a worksheet, or to write them up on the board, so that you don't even need to talk them through it. If latecomers are a problem for you, it is worth considering whether you should just start the lesson (preferably with a really engrossing task) so that when the students arrive late, they feel that they have missed out on something exciting. You can always discipline them later on in the lesson when the rest of the class are getting on with the work.

- *Create a partnership*: Teachers with a magic touch have the ability to make their children feel that the class is working in partnership with the teacher. This is very different to the mood in a classroom where the children must do what the teacher says, without any discussion or complaint. Creating this feeling of partnership is a complex process: it has to do with many of the aspects described above, such as your attitude, expectations, and a total refusal to give up on any child, no matter how badly they treat you. Teachers who create a partnership with their children also tend to adopt a very positive, even humorous approach, but without undermining their own authority. For more ideas on creating a positive feeling in your own classroom, see the chapter on 'The negative classroom'.

- *Observe your colleagues*: Possibly the best way in which we can develop our own teaching skills is to have the opportunity to observe our colleagues at work. This is especially so if you get the chance to watch a natural teacher in the classroom, and you are able to analyse and explore what he or she does to get such good results. Whatever stage of your career you are at, observations provide a very valuable experience. Whether you are an NQT or a teacher with years of classroom time under your belt, it really is worth asking your managers for the opportunity to watch a colleague you admire in the classroom. If you've just started at your school, and you're not sure who might provide an interesting and useful role model, then why not ask the children – they will be more than happy to let you know who their 'best' teachers are.

5 The little fidgets

Q. *My class are a bunch of little fidgets — they just can't seem to sit still! When they're sitting on the carpet to listen to a story or to do some whole-class work, I seem to spend half the time telling them off for wriggling about and not listening properly. They also get into conflicts with each other as they elbow and jostle for room on the carpet. When I set them an activity to be done at their desks, some of them spend more time shuffling in their seats, or getting up and wandering around the room, than actually working. They seem to find it impossible to focus properly on what I want them to do. Not only does this fidgeting and lack of concentration annoy me, but it's interfering with the quality of the work that they produce. How on earth do I get my children to learn to sit still and to develop better concentration?*

A. It can be really infuriating when children move around while you are trying to teach them. For a start, it is very distracting for a teacher who is trying to concentrate on delivering the lesson. It also suggests that the children are not focusing properly on the work you are doing, and the quality of their learning will certainly suffer if they cannot sit still and concentrate properly. For young children especially, sitting still and concentrating for extended periods of time is actually quite hard. Even in the secondary school, students who cannot stay still are a regular feature in classrooms. In my experience, there does seem to be a connection between those children who find it difficult to sit still, and those who find it hard to concentrate on their work. This would suggest that if we can find ways to get our 'little fidgets' to be less restless, we will also help our students develop their concentration skills and to focus on the tasks in hand.

One of the biggest problems with a class of fidgets is that it can lead to conflicts between the students. If a child bashes against his or her neighbour while shuffling around on the carpet, this can result in irritating tit-for-tat exchanges between the children about whose fault it is. These not only interfere with the learning that should be taking place, but also tend to make your classroom a place full of bad-tempered students. So much time can be wasted by these encounters, and the resulting low-level misbehaviour, that it is vital for the teacher to solve the issue.

Before we look at a variety of ways in which you can encourage stillness and focus in your children, it's a good idea to consider first exactly why some of our children find sitting still and concentrating such complex and challenging tasks. The majority of the reasons given below are areas on which the teacher can have a direct impact, either in terms of his or her own teaching approaches, or in other less direct ways. Your children may be fidgety or lacking in focus because of one specific factor described, or perhaps for a whole range of reasons, depending on the individual students.

- *Parental influences*: Children need to be 'trained', while they are young, in the art of focusing on one thing to the exclusion of any distractions, whether this is playing with a toy or completing a task of some type. If the parents or guardians have not got the child into the habit of sitting and focusing on one thing at a time, this can lead to a distracted and restless attitude in school as well. Lack of focus is not necessarily related to deprivation – a child who has far too many toys, but who is never taught to play with one single thing for any length of time, will also tend to lack concentration.

- *Distractions in the home*: Similarly, if a child is used to an easy diet of television or computer games, it is unlikely that he or she will find it easy to focus on something as apparently mundane as reading or writing. Excessive television and computer game use, with their bright colours and flickering images, tends to over-stimulate children. Consequently, when the child arrives at school, good concentration skills may be lacking. When we ask our children to concentrate on some of the more mundane learning tasks, which require high levels of focus, it is no wonder that they find it difficult to comply.

- *Excessive demands from the teacher*. Sometimes, the fault is with the teacher and not in the children themselves. We might demand that very young children sit still for long periods of time, when this is simply not a realistic expectation. Children do need to be given the opportunity to burn off their energy during the school day, rather than being asked to focus on a difficult activity for an extended period of time. This may mean that you need to learn how to break up your lessons or your teaching day into fairly small chunks of concentrated work time, with rest or activity sessions in between.

- *Lack of training*: It does take some time for any teacher to train his or her class into working in the way that is required in school and in the particular teacher's own classroom. This is just as true in the secondary school, as it is with the primary aged class. Although hopefully by the time they reach secondary level our students will have developed good concentration, we will also be asking them to complete more complex and lengthy activities and so they need to be trained in how this is done. Another issue with training your students is to do with your own personal preferences about the way that work should be done. When you first meet your children, you may be presenting them with a very different set of expectations and requirements from their previous teachers, and you will need to train them in working in the way that you want.

- *Lack of engagement with the work*: If your students do not find the work you set particularly interesting, exciting or relevant, it is far more likely that they will become restless and lose their focus during the lesson. Consider your own responses when you are listening to someone talk, perhaps in a staff meeting. If the speaker is dull, or if the content seems irrelevant to you, the temptation will be to lose your focus. I know from personal experience that I am inclined to mess around if a presentation is boring.

- *The time of day*: First thing in the morning, it could be that many of your children are still half asleep, and consequently less likely to be able to focus on work-related tasks (although conversely this sleepiness could mean that at least they are relatively still). Alternatively, it might be that morning is the time of day when some of them are at their liveliest. Much will depend on the individual children and on what goes on in their homes before they come to school, so you will need to take this into account. We have a natural dip in our levels of concentration and work rate in the early afternoon – the time when a siesta or nap is of great value (and actually used as a regular feature of the day in some schools on the continent). Of course, if you are having to teach your children at this time of the day, their concentration is going to be low and their ability to focus poor. This will probably result in a lot of that irritating fidgeting.

- *What the children eat/drink*: You may have noticed that your children find it particularly difficult to sit still just after break or lunch time. It could well be that they have been consuming fizzy drinks which are high in caffeine, and which can result in excessively high energy levels. Alternatively they may be consuming junk foods with high sugar contents, and consequently have a burst of sugar-based energy just as they arrive at your class, which quickly burns itself out.

- *The classroom environment*: If your room is excessively hot or cold, or perhaps very cramped and uncomfortable, it is inevitable that this will have an impact on the way that your children work and behave. No-one enjoys being made to work in an unsuitable environment, so this could well be a factor in the behaviour of the 'little fidgets'. For instance, in the primary classroom the carpet area where the children sit may be too small. If the students are all cramped together, this will inevitably lead to fidgeting and even conflicts, as they bang against each other in their attempts to get comfortable.

So, the first step in solving this issue is to establish exactly what the source of the problem is, or the range of reasons why the children are lacking in concentration and fidgeting excessively. You can then focus on improving your children's concentration skills, your lesson delivery, the classroom environment, or whichever factors apply in your case. Here are some suggestions as to how you might do this.

- *The use of targets*: When you do wish to develop your students' ability to sit still, or to encourage better levels of concentration, the setting of specific targets (and the rewarding of appropriately on-target behaviour) will prove invaluable. For instance, you might challenge your children to sit completely still for the whole of the time that it takes you to call out the register. You can then reward the class as a whole for achieving this target. Bear in mind that the reward that you give does not necessarily have to be a material one, such as stickers or merit marks, it might be as simple as lots of praise for their good behaviour. Generally speaking, children do love to please their teachers, so take full advantage of this.

- *The use of names*: Using a child's name is one of the easiest ways to gain his or her attention and to encourage the individual to behave as you wish. The effective teacher gets into the habit of always using the children's names when they are to be addressed. Sometimes there will be just a few individuals in a class who find it particularly hard to concentrate and stay still. If this is the case, try using their names with more frequency to ensure that the children focus on what you are saying for all or most of the time. A simple directed comment, such as '*Jodie, I'd love to see how still you can sit during this activity*', could be enough to get Jodie doing what you want.

- *A gradual build-up*: There is no point in expecting a sudden change from fidgety, restless and off-task behaviour, to impeccably behaved and completely focused children. If your problem is a class of little fidgets, you will need to build your way up gradually towards more stillness and better concentration. You could try setting targets of increasing length: for instance, the first week you might simply ask for complete stillness during the register, developing this in the next week to complete stillness while you read the class a story, and so on, building up the length of time and the expectation gradually.

- *Teach them appropriate behaviour*: Many children, especially the youngest ones, will not understand what you actually want and how it is that you expect them to behave. The teacher should share detailed information about appropriate behaviour with the class, training the children to behave as required, and practising the relevant behaviours over and over again. For instance, with reception-age children you might ask them to practise sitting on the carpet with legs crossed and arms folded, so that there is no chance of them banging against each other and setting off conflicts. For older, junior school, or secondary aged children, my expectations would be that they do not 'rock back' on their chairs, keeping all four legs of the chair on the floor. I would also insist that they stay seated unless they have permission to get up. In fact, this would be one of the very first behaviour expectations that I discuss with a class, and I would insist very firmly that they fulfil this requirement.

- *Teach them how to focus*: Concentration, and the stillness which accompanies it, are not necessarily natural skills for anyone, but they can be taught by the use of focus exercises. These exercises are designed to focus the children in on themselves and the work they are doing, almost like a form of meditation. As well as helping your students learn how to focus, these exercises will assist you in getting your class to listen to you in silence. They will also help the children to relax themselves in preparation for working (or at the beginning or end of lesson time). Below are just a few examples that you could try with your children. Notice how, in many of these exercises, the students are asked to close their eyes – this is helpful because it shuts out the myriad distractions of the normal classroom and allows them to concentrate fully on the activity.

- *Countdown*: Ask the class to close their eyes then count backwards from 50 to 0 in their heads. When they get to zero, they should open their eyes and prepare to start work. This activity encourages stillness as the children focus in on the task that you have asked them to complete.
- *Mental spelling*: Again, with eyes closed, the children spell different words in their heads. For instance, you might ask them to spell out their full names in their minds, perhaps seeing the individual letters being written down. Asking them to do this backwards can also prove very effective, as it makes the task more difficult, needing even greater levels of concentration.
- *Listening*: With their eyes shut, the children listen to all the sounds they can hear, starting inside the classroom, then gradually moving to sounds in the corridor and the school outside.
- *Statues*: The class are challenged to freeze as still as statues – they are allowed to breathe, but they must not move any part of their bodies. They must even keep their eyes still with no blinking (they can shut them if they want). The teacher sets a time target to make the exercise more of a challenge, for instance 2 minutes of complete and total stillness. The teacher then says '*3 ... 2 ... 1 ... freeze*' and the statues time begins. The length of time that you give can gradually be lengthened, as the children get better at the activity. This is a particularly good exercise for starting or finishing a lesson. You might also like to use it when you are calling the register. Note: if you have an appropriate classroom space you could get the children lying down to make the statue time more relaxing.

- *Set a challenge*: I find that children respond particularly well to the teacher who sometimes uses a fairly competitive manner to challenge them to behave appropriately. For instance, in the secondary school you might tell your Year 9 class that Year 7 can do 2 minutes of the statues exercise described above, and so you are challenging them to do 3 minutes. You will find them very keen to 'out-statue' their younger counterparts! If you teach the same primary class each day, you can challenge your children to achieve a better result than the previous day, for instance saying, '*You were quite still during the register yesterday, but today I challenge you to be completely frozen still for the whole time while I'm calling the names*'.

- *Clear the decks*: Often, restless children will tend to mess around with the things that they have on their desks, such as pens, books and so on. Of course, it's pretty much impossible for your children to fidget if there's nothing for them to fidget with (although some of them will still find a way!). So, when you want your class's full attention, for instance when you are explaining the work, ensure that there is nothing on the desks that might distract them. It is a very good idea to train them to start the lesson with a clear desk, and to keep their pens, books, pencil cases and so on in their bags until the time comes to work. Once you train them in the habit of having a clear desk, they will come to do this automatically at the start of class.

- *Keep 'teacher talk' to a minimum*: Many teachers, including me, do have the habit of talking more than is strictly necessary. If your class are a bunch of restless little fidgets, then expecting them to listen to you for extended periods of time is asking a great deal. Instead, put the focus of the work back on the children, at least some of the time. For instance, you might set worksheet or group activities that require very little input from the teacher, so that the students can get down to work straight away at the start of class. I do generally recommend that secondary school teachers get into the habit of taking the register at the start of the lesson, to pull the class together, and prepare them for work. However, if you find that the children are unable to keep still while you do this, it might be worth getting them started on the work, and then taking the register once they are settled.

- *Break up the work*: If your class is going to be asked to work for an extended stretch of time, it is a very good idea to break up the work by the use of quick physical activities. This helps prevent the restlessness that does inevitably occur when children are asked to sit still and work for long periods of time. For instance, after a period of work you might get your class to stand up and stretch their arms above their heads several times. Alternatively, you might use the exercise where you touch one hand to your nose and the other to your ear, and then alternate these as quickly as you can. This is not only a physical activity, but also requires a high level of mental agility.

- *Think about when you do what you do*: As I discussed earlier in this section, there are certain times of day when we are at our most alert and other times when our energy and concentration levels dip. Think carefully about when you ask your students to do different activities, and consider whether these are taking place at the most appropriate time. For instance, after lunch it may be a good idea to do some fairly calm and relaxing work, to take advantage of the post-lunch dip in energy. Similarly, don't attempt to do anything requiring high levels of concentration last thing on a Friday, when the children are tired from their week at school.

- *Adapt the physical environment*: If environmental factors within your classroom are contributing to your children's lack of concentration, then consider how you might make changes to improve things. For instance, if the room gets very hot and sunny, you might find that your children are very lethargic. If this is the case, ask the relevant manager whether blinds can be installed, pointing out that this is to facilitate a better learning environment. If the desks and chairs are very crowded within your classroom, you will probably find that any fidgeting quickly leads to conflicts, as the students crash into each other. If you do have this problem, then consider whether you can lay the room out in another way to create more of a feeling of space.

- *Encourage water consumption*: Research has suggested that many of our school children are actually dehydrated, and that this has an impact on their ability to concentrate. Suggest, to the powers that be, that your school invests in a water cooler to keep the children well hydrated. Alternatively, why not encourage your students to bring their own bottles of water into the classroom. Hopefully this will also help if the problem of restlessness is caused by over-consumption of fizzy and sugary drinks.

In the initial question, the teacher also mentions a problem with keeping the children in their seats once the work has been set. In many ways, this is a discipline issue rather than having anything to do with developing the students' concentration levels. With the majority of children, I would suggest a very simple but strict strategy for dealing with the problem. Essentially, the strategy comes down to the child making a straightforward choice about his or her own behaviour.

- If a student wishes to leave his or her seat for whatever reason, the child must raise a hand and have the teacher's permission before getting up.

- If a student does leave his or her seat without the teacher's express permission, an instant sanction (for instance a 5 minute detention) will be earned.

This simple choice between doing as the teacher wishes, or earning a specific punishment, makes life very straightforward for your children and for you. Explain the new regime very clearly before you start to apply it, and the students will have nothing to complain about if they do decide to break the rules, and consequently get punished. You may find yourself handing out a number of detentions in the early days of applying this strategy, but so long as you are consistent in giving the sanction and ensuring it is served, you will quickly find that the children decide against making the wrong choice.

In some very extreme situations, a student with special needs will actually find it practically impossible to stay in his or her seat for an entire lesson, and will have a tendency to get up (perhaps without realizing it) and wander around the room. In these cases it can prove very effective to set a quick target for the student at the start of each lesson. '*Okay David, today I want you to aim to stay in your seat for at least 10 minutes at a time. For every 10 minutes you stay in your seat, I'll come and give you one of these fantastic stickers.*' The target length of time can be extended each lesson, as the child develops the ability to stay still. By using a specific target, and rewarding the student for achieving it, you should quickly develop his or her ability to comply with your request.

6 The class from hell

Q. *I teach one class who, if I'm honest, are just a bunch of psychos. I dread the day every week when I'm due to teach them (if you can even call it teaching.) The night before I see them, I feel really ill and I can't sleep. The thought that I'm going to have to teach them the next day goes over and over in my mind and I just can't stop thinking about it. Sometimes I'm tempted to call in sick to school, so that I can avoid having to teach them for another week. It's not just that they won't do what I say, I could cope with that. It's that they're totally out of control – they run around the room, throw things at each other, and generally cause mayhem. I feel so embarrassed about my lack of control over these kids. What must everyone else think? I dread the day that the head teacher happens to come in the room when I'm teaching them. What on earth can I do?*

A. Does this situation sound familiar to you? It certainly does to me! I'm not ashamed to say that I've found myself in a similar position with some classes during my teaching career, despite the fact that I consider myself to be a good and effective teacher. During that difficult first NQT year as a teacher, it can sometimes feel like every day is spent facing the class from hell, but I have also experienced a similar problem further on in my career, when starting a job at a new school. Unfortunately, facing such difficult classes can make us start to doubt our own abilities as teachers, and this quickly leads us into a downward spiral in which we lose all confidence in our classrooms. And it's not long before the kids pick up on this lack of confidence, and consequently begin behaving even worse, to wind us up further.

So, why exactly is it that sometimes we have to face the class from hell? And what is it that makes children behave in this way? If you have to face the class from hell, it may be for a single specific reason, or there may be a number of factors at play. Being able to identify exactly what it is that is going wrong will not only help you in the search for possible solutions, but will also help you feel more confident that the problem is not necessarily of your own making. Below you will find a list that gives some of the reasons why your children might be behaving in this way. Consider which of these issues is causing the difficulties in your own situation, then look at the strategies that follow, to see if you can find some solutions to your own particular problem.

- *Subject-related issues*: In some cases, the subject being taught will be the cause of the problem. In the primary school, it might be that your class becomes extremely difficult when you have to teach them Maths; in the secondary school it could be that your students have an issue with their perception of certain subject areas, for instance Modern Foreign Languages. Perhaps inevitably, our students view some subjects as more 'cool' or interesting than others. It is often the case that a subject which is more active or practical will be seen as preferable to one in which they are required to write a great deal. You might have noticed how some academically weak children, whose struggle to learn tends to manifest itself in misbehaviour, actually enjoy and do very well in areas such as PE or Drama. In these subjects the fact that they are not being asked to work in an area where they are weak, such as literacy, means that they can actually enjoy their work and get a positive feeling of success.

- *Whole school issues*: If your children are this difficult to teach, bear in mind that whole school behaviour problems are probably playing a significant factor in the situation that you face. In a well ordered school, the students will be aware of the systems that are in place to deal with their behaviour. In this type of school, the children might still be tempted to misbehave with particular teachers, for instance a less than strict teacher, a supply or student teacher, or an NQT. However, they will be aware that the school has systems for dealing with the problem and that they will not be able to escape the consequences of their actions. On the other hand, in a school where behaviour is a real whole school issue, the ethos of the students may well be that 'we can get away with mucking around'. If this is the case for you, then your battle to get good behaviour is doubly difficult, and you will need plenty of support to resolve the problem.

- *Specific class or student issues*: If you work in a secondary school and you find yourself facing the class from hell, it is well worth asking around to see whether other teachers also view this particular class as being very difficult. It might be that the issues are with a specific class, or with a particular group of students within that class. If you do find yourself in this situation, at least you can console yourself that the problem is at least partially with the children, and not wholly with you as a teacher.

- *Specific groupings*: In the secondary school, class groupings are made up in a number of different ways. The class you teach might be formed from one tutor or form group, but it might also be a group that is set by ability, or formed in some other way. My experience has been that some year groups do prove to be more difficult or problematic than others – perhaps there was something in the air in the year that they were born! (Or perhaps, more likely, there has been some kind of problem with a weak head of year, or perhaps with poor teaching in the past, or a lack of continuity of staff.)

- *New to the school*: Whether you're an NQT or an experienced teacher, difficulties with behaviour can often arise when you start at a new school. The children have no previous experience of you, and consequently they are more likely to try you out when it comes to their classroom behaviour. In addition, you will be uncertain as yet about how the behaviour policies and systems work at your new school, and the children may pick up on this air of uncertainty.

- *A lack of confidence*: In my experience, students quickly pounce on a teacher who is lacking in confidence. If you find behaviour management difficult, this can transmit itself to the class (perhaps subconsciously, through an overly negative or defensive approach). Sadly, once the children pick up on a teacher who lacks confidence, it is far more likely that they will become out of control and turn into the class from hell.

- *The ringleader:* Occasionally, a class will have one student in it who acts as a ringleader, and who has a very strong influence on the other children's behaviour. Often, these students tend to be physically advanced, bigger or more mature than their peers. Sometimes the influence is as a result of fear – the ringleader is a bit of a bully; other times it is the fact that they have a certain charisma and self-confidence which appeals to their less secure classmates.

Once you have identified what the specific problem (or group of problems) is with your own class from hell, the next step is to explore exactly what you can do about it. Teaching these kinds of groups can lead to very high levels of stress for the teacher. It is therefore essential that you do resolve the issue, otherwise you may find yourself struggling for the entire school year, and getting increasingly unhappy in your job. Below are some practical ideas for dealing with the really difficult class. I have focused my discussion on each of the difficulties identified above, suggesting what you might do to resolve each type of problem in turn.

- *Subject-related issues:* If the problem is to do with a specific subject the key is, logically, to try to make that area of the curriculum more appealing to the class. Take the time to find out what really motivates your children, particularly the type of subjects and activities that they enjoy. You could do this by chatting with other members of staff, by simply observing your children at work, or by asking the students what they most like doing. Once you have identified the best motivators for the class, try to deliver the subject you are teaching using these areas of the curriculum. For instance, if the children in the class from hell are very keen on computers, get yourself booked into the computer room asap! Alternatively, if the students love practical curriculum areas such as Drama or Art, then focus on a more creative approach to the subject in question.

- *Whole school issues*: It can be very difficult for the individual teacher to resolve behaviour problems in a school where there is no strong ethos of good behaviour. The children see other classes getting away with poor behaviour and, consequently, they feel that this is the way that they can behave too. If you find yourself in this situation, there are a number of useful steps you can take:
  - *Set an example*: If you are working in a challenging school, where poor behaviour is the norm, then work on making your own classroom a haven of good behaviour. Set up a psychological barrier between your own working environment and the rest of the school and refuse to allow low expectations to intrude.
  - *Don't get angry, be surprised*: If the children do choose to misbehave for you, the natural immediate reaction is, of course, to get angry with them. However, in a school where poor behaviour is the norm, this is actually rather unfair on the children (as well as not being a particularly effective response by the teacher). My advice is, instead of becoming angry with them, to try to respond with surprise when they do muck around. Your reaction should suggest an attitude of '... but you're such lovely children, I expect you to behave well, why aren't you doing this?' (even where this is completely untrue!).
  - *Create a policy of your own*: If there is no whole school behaviour policy in place in your school, or if the one you are expected to use doesn't really work, then why not make up one of your own? Decide on a very clear set of expectations and rules, plan a series of sanctions and rewards that you will stick to, and then go through this carefully and in detail with your children. Then they will have some sense of certainty and continuity, even if this is only in your classroom.
  - *Fight for what you believe*: Although it's hard to do, if you are really determined to get good behaviour, and you fight for what you want, then it will pay off in the end (although be

warned, it could take some time). Work at applying your 'policy' in a very clear and structured way, fighting to achieve your expectations, no matter how long it takes. Eventually the children will see that, in your classroom at least, good behaviour is expected and rewarded.

- *Specific class or student issues/specific groupings*: If you work in a secondary school, and the issue is with specific classes, students or groupings, then do be aware that you are probably not alone. There may well be many other teachers in your school experiencing difficulties with the class from hell, and this fact alone should help alleviate the stress that your situation is probably causing you. There are a number of useful steps which you can take to make your life more bearable when a particular group of children are causing you difficulties.
  - *Discover the extent of the problem*: When you're coping with the class from hell, it can really help, as I pointed out above, to simply know that others are also experiencing problems. Ask around the school about the children you find difficult – does anyone (or everyone) else have the same experience of them? If you do find that this is the case, what strategies are the other members of staff using to deal with the situation?
  - *Get the management to sort it*: If the problem does turn out to be a school-wide one, then a useful approach is to gang together as a group of teachers (there's strength in numbers), and approach the management to see whether there is anything that can be done. For instance, a particular group of very difficult students might be split up from each other, perhaps being moved into different form groups. It is, of course, the responsibility of the management of a school, as well as of the teachers, to ensure that the classroom behaviour you face is appropriate and acceptable.
  - *Use a seating plan*: Often, when a small group of students are causing problems, the answer can simply be to not let them sit together. Why not draw up a seating plan in which the 'bad' children are placed next to their 'good'

counterparts, and see whether this works for you? If you feel unconfident about whether the students will agree to sit in the places you have allocated, then request that a senior manager attends the start of your lesson to ensure that they comply. A useful time to instigate a seating plan is at the start of a new term, when you can also decide to approach the class with a new and stricter persona.

- *Watch out for the 'self-fulfilling prophecy'*: Sometimes, when a particular class gets a name for itself, the teachers start expecting them to behave badly. This expectation quickly becomes a self-fulfilling prophecy, because teachers approach the students with negative feelings already in place and, consequently, become more defensive with them than they might otherwise be. When this happens, the students seem to behave badly simply to show us just how bad they really can be.

- *Grin and bear it*: Sadly, in some situations, it could be that you just have to grin and bear it with a particularly difficult group. Keep it in mind that, at the end of the year, you should (hopefully) get rid of them. In the meantime, try to see your class from hell as a learning experience, a chance to hone your behaviour management skills, and to try out all those strategies that you might not otherwise use.

- *New to the school*: When you start work at a new school, whether as an NQT or as a more experienced teacher, it is inevitable that it will take you a while to learn the new systems, to suss out your class or classes, and to discover which children are going to cause you problems. Unfortunately, it is during this short space of time that your students might decide that they can take advantage of your lack of certainty. Before the first term starts, talk to other staff to find out whether you are going to be teaching any particularly difficult children or classes. If you are, approach these groups with a very firm hand right from the start. Find out, too, the name of a manager who is willing to support you in behaviour management, preferably someone who the students fear or respect. Although I don't generally agree with using another teacher's name to encourage good behaviour, in some cases it is very useful to be able to say, *'If you do that again, I'll have to speak to Mr/Miss X about your behaviour'*.

- *The ringleader*: There are certainly some children who seem to have a 'hold' over a class, and who can turn what would have been a relatively well-behaved group of students into the class from hell. I've experienced this situation myself on a number of occasions in the past, and have developed a range of strategies to try to resolve the problem. Much will depend on the particular circumstances you find yourself in and the nature of the individual with whom you are dealing. Here are some ideas for you to try.
  - *Isolate the troublemaker*: One approach that can work well is to isolate the ringleader, because this helps keep him or her from influencing the other children in a negative way. You might organize this yourself, or you could ask that other staff help you instigate some form of isolation. In the primary school, this might mean the child working with a classroom assistant on individual tasks; in the secondary school it could be that the student is moved to another group, either permanently or on a temporary basis. One technique I have seen used to very good effect is for a difficult student, in a lower year group, to be put in to work with a much older class. For instance, a Year 8 child could sit in with an A level group. The older students are highly unlikely to allow a youngster to disrupt them and they may provide a good influence for the difficult child.
  - *Be a tough cookie*: Another idea is to be very hard on the student (and the class as a whole). Apply sanctions in a very clear and structured way, and take every step you can to discipline the child, until you find out what works best in the specific circumstances. This might involve phoning the parents, 'red card'-ing the student, or using any other ultimate sanction that you have available.
  - *Develop a relationship*: If you suspect that the ringleader might be amenable given time, then why not work on

developing a relationship with him or her? Often, these students are actually putting up a front for their peers, and in fact they will respond very well if the teacher makes the effort to get to know them. Show that you are tough but fair – you want everyone to learn, and that's why you insist on good behaviour. Eventually, your ringleader may respond to this approach.

The following are some more general tips about ways that the teacher can deal with the class from hell. These ideas focus on the teacher's feelings in this type of situation and ways in which you can help yourself survive. The strategies I give will help stop you from feeling like a failure and also help you start to go about the long, often difficult, process of actually teaching and controlling these children. One of the most important things is to avoid getting stressed, because this can lead to a defensive attitude: these techniques will help you achieve this.

- *Keep a perspective*: In this sort of situation, it is very easy (and natural) to start becoming defensive and blaming yourself, quickly losing any sort of perspective. The next time you teach the class, after the lesson (and after you've had a bit of time to recover from the experience), take some time to step back and consider the class as a whole. Is it really true that every single child in the class is causing trouble, or is the problem limited to a group of individuals? Once you examine this in a rational way, you will probably find that it is a maximum of five or so students who are making your life impossible. Of course, others may have been influenced by these children and may have started to join in with the poor behaviour, but in reality the majority of students we teach do actually want to learn and behave properly. If you can keep a perspective about how big the problem actually is in reality, you will help yourself deal with things in a more rational way. You will also find yourself more able to focus on the good kids, rather than the bad ones (see below for more thoughts about this technique).

- *Don't take it personally*: When a class refuses to behave for you, or to do as you wish, it is very tempting to start taking the behaviour personally. You then get yourself into a position where you get wound up very easily, and become incapable of dealing with the issue in a calm and rational way. The feeling that the children are 'picking on you' is natural, but is, in fact, unlikely to be accurate. Again, try to step back from the way the class is behaving – this will help you solve the problem in as relaxed a way as possible. The more relaxed you can be when faced with the class from hell, the less defensive you will become and the better your children will respond.

- *Don't be afraid to opt out*: Sometimes, it will prove necessary for your own sanity to opt out of teaching a class like this, at least for a little while. In fact, it could be that the children are so badly behaved that they are putting themselves in danger, or that they are making you so tense and angry that there is no telling what might happen if you do lose your temper completely. In this position, don't worry about the teaching – it's a straightforward case of survival. I'm not suggesting that you stop turning up at school, but what you can do is make life as easy as possible for yourself when you do have to face these children. It might be that you decide to book the class into the computer room for the remainder of the term and set them a worksheet to do while they are in there. Put even the most horrendous of children in front of a computer and they will normally, at the very least, stay in their seats. You may be worried that you won't be able to keep them on-task (and in fact you probably won't if they are this difficult to teach). I would recommend that you simply don't worry about it – your main priority is simply to get through the lesson. If they want to log on to the Internet, then view it as an educational experience and don't beat yourself up about it!

- *Develop a sense of partnership*: I like to feel that I have a partnership with my students – I insist on good behaviour simply because it is what is best for them. I want them to learn and I will achieve this in any way I possibly can. However, I always try to retain a sense of perspective – I understand that sometimes they simply won't want to work hard and, as long as they balance this with good work most of the time, I'm happy. With a class from hell, especially if it contains very disaffected students, you need to work out exactly how much 'hard work' you're going to be able to get from them and how best to go about it. For instance, you might trade 10 minutes of very hard work for a 5-minute chat break, making it clear to the children that they must fulfil their side of the bargain. Alternatively, if you do decide to work in the computer room, you could turn a blind eye to any off-task Internet use, as I suggested above, but make it very clear to the students that you know it's going on. Show them that you are 'letting' them get away with it, so long as they get their work done. This will help them develop respect for you, and a partnership with you: the message you want to give is that they can't get one over on you, but that you are willing to be a little bit relaxed if they are also willing to play the game.

- *Focus on the good kids*: When we're working with really difficult children, it is very tempting to focus on the badly behaved ones, simply because they demand most of our attention to keep them in order. However, giving them attention in this way is, in most cases, a mistake, because it simply reinforces any attention-seeking behaviour. At all times, do keep reminding yourself that there are some very well-behaved, good and decent children in every class, no matter how difficult the class might seem. By opting out from the stress of trying to discipline (and even teach) the really abusive students, you will allow the decent kids a chance to get something done. Don't feel guilty about having to resort to these tactics for survival – sometimes it is just the best thing you can do for the majority of your children.

- *Insist that steps are taken*: As I pointed out above, teachers should not be expected to put up with excessively poor behaviour, especially if the problem involves a whole class, or most of the students in one class. If you are an NQT, you are especially entitled to help and support when you are in a situation such as the one described. It is of course important to insist that something is done about the problem, not only because it makes your life difficult, but also because the students' learning will be suffering as a result of the poor behaviour. Talk to a manager, perhaps a head of year, head of department or deputy head. Insist that something is done, for instance the worst three offenders could be taken out of the class to make a point to them, or a manager could come into your lessons to support you for a time.

- *Use a range of behaviour management strategies*: When you are having a real problem with a class, it is time to put a wide range of techniques into position, working through different approaches until you find some that work in your own situation. You can find a whole host of useful behaviour management strategies in my book *Getting the Buggers to Behave* (2001, London: Continuum). You can also find some tips that you should find useful in the chapter at the beginning of this book on 'The talkative class'.

7 The balanced relationship

Q. *I teach in a really lovely school, and most of my children are great kids. I believe it's really important that they like and respect me, as well as me just being their teacher. The problem is, I'm worried that if I get too close to them, they won't do as I say anymore, and I'll lose control of them. On the other hand, I don't want to be one of those really strict teachers who shouts all the time, and who the kids hate. Sometimes, I'll do a really fun activity with my class to get them to like me more, but then they get over excited and start to push at the limits of what is allowed. How can I achieve a balanced relationship with my children?*

A. Understandably, teachers can often feel a bit confused about their role – to what extent are they the children's friend, and how far are they simply their teacher? Essentially, teachers take on a role that combines many different features – educator, social worker, counsellor, parental figure, friend and so on. We spend a great deal of time with our students and we do, of course, develop some deep and often lasting relationships, perhaps ones that might continue over a number of years. The best teachers find a way to combine the two roles – they genuinely like and get on with their students, but they never step too far outside their professional role. It's finding the right balance that is so difficult, especially if you are working with really lovely kids.

The first time that a child comes to ask for your advice, or to cry on your shoulder, can make a teacher feel rather proud and special. The same applies at the end of term, when you are showered with gifts and cards, which all tell you what a wonderful person you are. It is very easy to get carried away and to allow your relationship with your class or classes to become overly relaxed and friendly. However, if you do choose to get too pally with your children, this can lead to problems in the long term. For instance, if you suddenly find that you need to crack down on some behaviour issues that have arisen, this will be much harder to do if your children view you mainly as their friend, rather than as the slightly more authoritative figure of a teacher.

Another potentially complicated scenario is when one child becomes particularly attached to you, perhaps because of a difficult home life in which he or she doesn't get much love or affection. In these instances you do need to pull away from the situation a little, making it clear that you are, above all, the child's teacher (although of course a very caring one). It is important at all times to bear your professional role in mind, and not to allow the idea of favourites or 'special' children to influence your work and your manner within the classroom.

In addition to the problems encountered by the teacher who wants to become the children's friend, it can also be very tempting to provide your students with lots of fun and free spirited lessons, in the hope that this will make them like you. However, as you can see from the question above, this may lead to problems with your classroom control. I am definitely not saying that learning should not be fun (of course it should be). Unfortunately, though, it is often the case that when children are given too much freedom and excessively exciting activities, they will tend to stretch the limits in the assumption that anything goes. This is especially so when you are first establishing your relationship with a class, because the children will be unsure about where the boundaries are. The thoughts and ideas below will help you to find and maintain the right balance with your own children.

- *Understand your children's needs and perceptions*: Children tend to have quite fixed views of what teachers are and should be. What they generally want and need is for you to be their teacher, not their friend, parent or big brother/sister. Although you might believe that they would like you to be 'one of them', taking such an approach is, in fact, likely to have the effect of confusing them about your respective roles. Think carefully about how your children want and need to perceive you – they will feel far more secure, and consequently learn and behave much better, if they view you as a slightly distant figure. Above all else, you should be seen to care most about their educational success and take every step you can to ensure that this happens for each and every one of them.

- *Consider what you're there for*: Although the teacher is obviously an important factor in a child's socialization and emotional development, at the end of the day your primary role as a professional is to help your children learn. Focus on this aspect of your job and, if you do it properly, you'll find that the children respect (and most probably like) you as a person. Your focus is best put on making the learning the most valuable experience it can possibly be, providing engaging and interesting activities which help your children to learn in the best way you know how.

- *Provide a suitable, adult role model*: Teachers offer their students a very valuable role model of how adults can and should work, behave and treat other people. For some children who come from a background of poor parenting skills, this appropriate adult role model is probably missing at home. It is therefore doubly important that you offer these individuals someone to look up to and to learn from. You may find that children from a less than suitable home life do become excessively attached to you, seeing you almost as a surrogate parent. Although you will obviously want to be caring towards these children, it is your duty as a professional to keep a reasonable distance, so that they learn how to interact properly with the adults in their lives. Remember that, at the end of the year, 'your' children will most probably become someone else's class – don't make your relationship with them so close that it becomes difficult for them to leave you behind.

- *Understand the meaning of and reasons behind respect*: Every teacher wants their children to respect them, but being respected is not necessarily the same as being liked (although the two can obviously exist simultaneously). Respect comes from a number of different areas in the teacher's personality and practice. First, the children see that you want to teach them as well as you are able, and that your primary purpose is to help them develop to the best of their ability and learn as much as they possibly can. Second, you will gain respect if you treat your students as proper people, as fully rounded individuals, and not 'just' kids who must simply do as you say irrespective of how they think and feel. For instance, when you are setting rules for your classroom, it is worthwhile spending the time to consult your class about what they feel are suitable guidelines for good work and behaviour. By giving them ownership of the rules in this way, they will see that you view them as important individuals who have a right to comment on what happens in your classroom. Finally, to gain respect your children need to sense and understand your enthusiasm for the job, and your passion for the subject or subjects that you teach. If your teaching is filled with energy and enjoyment, and you enthuse about the work that you set, then they will respect you for the way you do your job.

- *It's not about like and dislike*: One of the dangers with getting too close to your children is that you might end up having 'favourites' – giving those students who you like best more attention, and treating them with more leniency if they do misbehave. Children quickly sense when this is happening, and they view it as extremely unfair when they see a teacher being biased towards certain students, which of course it is. Naturally, teachers will like some children more than others, because we are human beings, and we have our own personal preferences and our own individual characters. However, in the classroom it's not about whether you like or dislike your children, it's about getting them to learn as well as they can. I know from personal experience that there are some students that I really like as people and others that, if I'm honest, I don't like very much at all. However, it's essential that we, as teachers, keep our own feelings out of the equation and that we treat all our children in the same way.

- *Keep it calm*: In the question, the teacher mentions doing 'fun activities' to get the children to 'like' him. Of course, it is vital to get the children engaged in the learning process, but it's also important to differentiate between what makes an engaging activity and what is simply fun for the sake of it. Although you might feel that I'm being a bit of a killjoy, there are a number of problems with using a 'fun' (i.e. over-exciting) lesson:

  - It can lead to a class full of extremely over-excited children.
  - It potentially might result in poor behaviour.
  - There may be problems ensuring the children's safety if they are running about or generally getting out of control.
  - The teacher will tend to get rather frazzled by the chaos.
  - The children may come to expect that all their lessons will be 'fun' and, consequently, refuse to do more serious, boring work when it is necessary.
  - In the primary classroom, the teacher has to calm the children down when it's time for some quiet work.
  - In the secondary classroom, you will not be popular with other staff if they have to teach the over-excited class next lesson!

How, then, do you go about keeping a calm atmosphere in the classroom? Here are some tips:

  - When introducing an activity that you know the children will see as fun, take the time to set the work in a calm manner. Use a quiet and relaxed tone of voice and give the instructions about what you want the class to do, slowly and in clear detail.
  - Make it clear that the children must stay settled and focused if they are to receive the reward of doing this particular lesson. Develop the idea of a partnership – you are kind enough to allow them to do a fun lesson, so they must respect this by behaving appropriately for you.
  - Warn the class that, if they start to get out of hand, you will simply stop the fun activities and revert to something else less exciting. Point out that you don't actually want to do this, but if they force you by their attitude, then you are quite willing to call a halt to the work.

- Greater control can be kept by making the fun work a whole class activity and asking for volunteers to demonstrate in front of the class. In this way the teacher can keep a lid on over-excited behaviour.

- *Keep the limits in place*: Sometimes, it is oh so tempting to relax the limits for a while, to allow the children to 'let off steam' and go a bit wild, in the hope that this will help them develop a good relationship with you. The problem with this is that your boundaries (or limits) need to be fixed, clear and definite, so that the children understand what is and isn't allowed in your classroom. If you relax the limits from time to time, what tends to happen is your children simply become completely confused and disorientated. With experience, you will start to see the sense behind keeping your limits firmly in place at all times. Your students need to know where they stand and they will appreciate it if the boundaries remain the same in every lesson, as this will help them feel secure.

- *Use humour*: Children love teachers who are able to have a laugh, both within the content and delivery of the lesson, and also at themselves when they do something silly. For instance, if you trip over in the classroom and your children laugh, it's important to be able to laugh along with them, rather than reacting in a defensive way or getting angry. This helps defuse any tension that you might feel. Remember, though, never to make jokes at a child's expense. The balance of power and authority in the classroom lies with the teacher and you should never take advantage of this by picking on a student when using humour.

- *Be in a consistent (or even good) mood*: Children do prefer it if their teachers are not too inconsistent in their moods. They like to know what to expect from the teacher when he or she comes into the classroom and, if this is different each day, it will be very confusing for the children. In fact it strikes me that our children probably prefer a teacher who is consistently in a strict or 'bad' mood, to one whose moods vary wildly from happy to angry and back again. Now, of course, we are only human beings and there will be occasions when we are feeling stroppy, or depressed, or excited, or tired, or any one of the whole spectrum of moods. However, if we do want our children to respect and like us, we need to present them with a consistent and relatively fixed persona. If you enjoy your work, and you show this through the good mood that you present to your class, then your children will respond by developing a balanced relationship with you.

- *Take a genuine interest*: Children seem to have an innate ability to tell whether an adult is really interested in them as individuals: in their achievement, their welfare, their personal development and so on. A teacher with a genuine interest in his or her children will find that a sense of partnership quickly develops with the class, and respect naturally flows from this in both directions. Take the time to listen to what your students have to say and what their interests are, not only as it concerns the work that you do, but also in terms of their lives outside of school.

- *Keep up-to-date on the latest trends*: Although I would not recommend that you pretend to be into the latest trends just to get in with your children, it is certainly worth keeping up-to-date with what's going on in the world that your students inhabit. With the very young this might mean knowing about the latest craze for a particular toy; with older students it could be that you take at least a passing interest in the names of the music groups that are in the charts. If you can at least show that you understand their interests beyond the classroom, your children will respond by developing a better relationship with you.

- *Show flexibility*: In my experience, children like teachers who are able to respond to their moods and individual needs in a flexible way. For instance, after a very hectic PE lesson late on a Friday afternoon, the class might not be in the right mood for an hour of writing in silence. There is little point, then, in insisting that the students take a long written test. If you can offer flexibility in such a situation, your children will develop greater respect for you as a teacher and as a person. Remember, the teacher who offers flexibility is not suggesting that the children are in control, or that they can get away without doing much work. Instead, you are showing that you can respond to the class and empathize with how they are feeling, at least some of the time. My advice is that you should always be prepared to throw your lesson plan out of the window, if you see that it really does not suit the mood of the class at a particular moment in time.

- *Get involved outside the classroom*: Some of the best relationships I've developed with students have been during extra curricular activities, such as a school drama production. In these situations, both the teacher and the child get the opportunity to be 'themselves' in a setting where much more individuality can be allowed. Do seize every chance you are offered to get involved with activities outside the classroom, as this will have an extremely beneficial effect on the quality of your relationships with your students. If you have an interest in sport, ask whether you can run a school team; if you have a secret hankering to be a set designer and builder, approach the teacher running the school play and offer your help. I can guarantee you, it will be gratefully received.

- *Know when it's appropriate to get close*: It is actually possible to develop a very close relationship with some classes, and it is important that you respect your own professional judgement so that you can see when this is appropriate. For instance, with an exceptionally well-motivated and well-behaved class, the teacher can afford to relax a little and show a bit more of his or her true persona to the students. The important thing is that the children still know where the limits are and that the work that they produce is done to the best of their ability. It is often possible to gradually relax with a class over time, so that by the third term of the school year your relationship has developed, becoming a little less formal as you go along.

8 The negative classroom

Q. *Although I started out the year on a very positive note, recently the atmosphere in my classroom has been going rapidly downhill. I feel that the children have developed a very negative attitude towards me, towards the work that I ask them to do and, in fact, towards school as a whole. They're always moaning that the activities are boring, or that they don't understand the tasks I set. I'm also noticing that their behaviour is degenerating – just small, low-level messing around, but it's really beginning to get on my nerves. If I had to use one word to describe their behaviour, it would be that they are developing an 'attitude'. As a consequence of all this, I've begun to approach my work in a very negative way and I come into school expecting the worst from them. What can I do to create a more positive feeling with my class?*

A. There are a whole range of reasons why a teacher might find (or indeed create) a negative atmosphere in his or her classroom. It could be that you are dealing with extremely troubled children, whose behaviour is so difficult that it infects the whole class and also begins to wear you down over time. It might be that you have simply been exhausted by the demands of the job and this is filtering through into your persona in the classroom, creating a negative undercurrent in the work that you do. It could be that you're an NQT and that you're finding your first year in the job really hard; alternatively it might be that you're a highly experienced teacher, and that you've simply become a little bit stale after years in the teaching profession.

Developing and maintaining a positive atmosphere in the classroom is, I believe, absolutely essential for effective teaching and for good behaviour management. Ideally, we want our children to come into the classroom feeling excited about what they are going to learn and fully enthused about the whole school experience. Sadly, some students do come into school with a very negative outlook and, in some cases, you may be fighting against this disaffection right from the start of the school year. If this is the situation that you find yourself in, the struggle to get the children to view their education positively could be a long and difficult one. Sometimes, it is things that the teacher is (probably subconsciously) doing that might have created a negative feeling with the children.

Although creating a positive atmosphere in your classroom takes hard work and often a great deal of energy, in the long run you will be making your life far easier. Once the students start to approach your lessons with a positive outlook, you will find that this has a knock-on effect, requiring less and less effort each time to recreate the good feelings from the past. You will also quickly develop a reputation in the school as a whole as a 'good' teacher whose classes are to be enjoyed and one for whom it is well worth behaving properly. The tips that I give below will help you in developing and maintaining a positive atmosphere in your own classroom.

- *Pace yourself*: The temptation is always to start the year with a big bang in terms of lesson preparation and in the way that you present the work to your class. Although we definitely want to engage and interest our children early on, you should guard against wearing yourself out at the start of the year. You could find that by the time the first half-term is finished, you are exhausted and unable to maintain the high standards you have set yourself. Getting overly tired can lead to a tendency to become negative with the children, so ensure that you pace yourself, particularly during the first term.

- *Set the standards early on*: It is tempting, particularly when we first start teaching, to be a little too lenient on low-level misbehaviour at the start of the year. You might feel that your children's behaviour is perfectly acceptable and not see the need to spend lots of time going through your expectations with them, or in being particularly strict. However, do ensure that you don't get lulled into a false sense of security as far as behaviour is concerned. If you do, you could find yourself suddenly faced with the type of behaviour described in the question. The problem is that having to then take a stricter approach with your class, when you started out so relaxed, may lead to negative attitudes within both the teacher and the students. The key is to set the standards you require early on and stick to them throughout your time with the class, only relaxing when you are completely sure that the children are fully under control.

- *Expect the best*: As I've said throughout this book, it is absolutely vital for the teacher to set up clear expectations about work and behaviour right from the start of the time with a class. As well as making your expectations completely clear, do also learn to expect the absolute best, both in terms of the work that your children produce and also in the way that they treat you and each other. A teacher who expects his or her children to work and behave in an exemplary manner and who reacts with surprise, rather than anger, when they do not, will create a very positive mood within the classroom.

- *Share the blame*: The teacher in the question above seems to place the blame for the problem firmly with the children, but this is not necessarily fair or true. In most instances, the teacher must share the responsibility when there is a negative atmosphere in the classroom. Consider whether your children might be picking up a negative mood from the way that you approach them, or whether you and your students are feeding off each other's unenthusiastic attitude to create a vicious cycle of bad feelings. If this is the case, remember that you are the adult, and that it is your responsibility, as a professional, to change your own attitude, as well as working on your children's attitudes in the classroom.

- *Mind your language*: The way that we talk to our children and the content of what we say, can have a huge impact on their attitude towards us and towards their learning. Think about the way that you speak, for instance when you are dealing with a behaviour problem. Do you use words like 'stupid' and phrases such as 'shut up'? Although it is all too easy for these terms to slip out (we are only human after all), if you do treat your children like this, then it is no wonder if they respond in a similarly rude and negative way. Consider also the way that you introduce the work – do you make it sound interesting and exciting, or dull and boring? Your own approach will be reflected in that of your students, so try to use language that suggests how wonderful the lessons will be.

- *Smile!*: When you're trying to create a positive atmosphere, please don't forget to smile at your children. Come into the room with a happy look on your face and this will immediately transmit your good feelings to the class about what is going to happen during the lesson. Smiling and laughing also helps relieve tension – it relaxes your face and helps you deal with any problems that do arise in a more positive manner.

- *Brighten up your room*: A negative atmosphere can be created or reinforced by our surroundings. If you work in a school where the environment is run-down and dilapidated, then this is bound to have an effect on your children (and on you as well). If this is the case, spend some time brightening up your room by creating colourful displays, or putting up bright posters. This will help detract from the overall negative feeling of your surroundings. Even if your class-room is already nicely decorated and well maintained, you can add to the positive sense that your students will get in your lessons by putting up displays and changing them regularly throughout the year. Displays also show that we are celebrating the work that our children produce, and again this will add to a positive feeling within the classroom.

- *Brighten up your teaching*: If your students are taking a negative attitude to the work, then it could be time to brighten up your teaching as well. This doesn't mean that every single lesson has to be an all-out singing and dancing extravaganza. However, you should aim to offer your children one or more lessons a week that are really fun and exciting. That way, you can re-enthuse them about their learning, as well as keeping yourself from getting stale and bored.

- *Give 'em a shock*: If you do find yourself dealing with a whole class of students who have taken on a negative attitude, then it is worth considering the value of giving them a shock. A surprise of some sort could help change their attitudes towards you, your classroom and the work that you do. It could also help you persuade them to take a new and fresh look at their learning environment. For instance, you might completely rearrange the furniture in your room, so that the class are facing in a completely different direction. Alternatively, you could come into a Science lesson dressed up as a mad professor and present the work in a crazy voice.

9 When sanctions don't work

Q. *I like to use sanctions to control the behaviour in my class, for instance setting a detention when a child isn't doing the work properly. The problem is that my students just don't seem to take me, or the punishments I give, seriously. Sometimes, a child will literally laugh in my face when I say that I'm giving out a detention. Alternatively, the student will complain that I'm being unfair, and that he or she doesn't actually deserve the punishment. Also, the children have a tendency to become very confrontational when I have to set detentions, and I find this very hard to cope with. I'm worried that this issue is damaging my status with the whole class. The other problem I'm experiencing is that when I do set detentions, the students simply don't turn up. How can I make sanctions work for me?*

A. The use of sanctions is certainly one route to gaining good behaviour and hard work from your children, but it's by no means the only way. When we are faced with a consistently poor attitude from our classes, it is all too tempting to dish out punishments to try and resolve the matter. To a certain extent, giving out these punishments is also a way for the teacher, probably subconsciously, to gain revenge on children who don't want to do what we ask. However, as the teacher in the question has noted, there are a number of difficulties inherent in the use of sanctions to control your classes. Although sanctions certainly have their place, and indeed can be a very effective behaviour management tool, it really is worth questioning how valuable they are in your own particular situation. Before we look at the use of sanctions in more detail, let's consider how and why problems occur when punishments are given in the classroom.

- *Confusion*: One of the main reasons why problems occur with the use of sanctions is when they have not been properly explained in advance. If a child is to be punished for doing something wrong, he or she must first understand that the behaviour in question is unacceptable, why this particular behaviour is not allowed and what the end results of behaving in this way will be (i.e. the sanction or other consequence). If this understanding is not in place, then it should be no surprise when the children become upset and claim that we are being unfair to them when we dish out punishments.

- *A negative feeling*: Sanctions do also have a tendency to create a very negative atmosphere in the classroom, and this is something that teachers obviously want to avoid. When children are constantly being sanctioned, they start to get the feeling that the classroom is a place of punishment, rather than of pleasure. Consequently, it becomes far more likely that confrontations and other negative encounters will occur between the teacher and his or her students. (For more thoughts about creating negative and positive atmospheres in your classroom, see the previous question and answer.)

- *Your teaching style*: If your immediate response to every child who doesn't do exactly as you wish is to dish out a punishment, it is likely that you will be using a very strict and indeed harsh style of teaching. Although this 'old school' style of teaching can be an effective method of controlling behaviour, it does tend to lead to confrontations. It is also very wearing on the teacher, who has to constantly set punishments, and ensure that they are served.

- *Inconsistency*: Another problem with sanctions is that there is a natural tendency within teachers to apply them in an inconsistent way. (And I do include myself in this statement.) For instance, we might focus on a child who we find particularly annoying, punishing him or her more harshly than our other students. Of course this may well be done subconsciously, but the children will still pick up on it.

They then start to resent a teacher who seems to be treating them unfairly, and a negative cycle of complaints and confrontations is set in motion. It is surprisingly hard to fight against this inconsistency within yourself, but it is essential that you treat all children the same if sanctions are going to work.

- *A public punishment*: When we set a punishment in class, it is all too tempting to respond in the heat of the moment and to shout out the sanction across the crowded classroom. '*Right, that's it, I've had enough of your stupid behaviour! You've got an hour's detention with me after class.*' Herein lies another of the difficulties with the use of sanctions. Is it any wonder if a child, faced with the embarrassment of being punished so publicly in front of his or her peers, responds by laughing off the threat? Alternatively, and even worse in terms of your standing in front of the class, the child might decide to take you on, becoming abusive and refusing to do as you ask.

- *The need to follow through*: Another issue with the use of sanctions, particularly that of detentions, is that they *must* be served if they are to prove an effective way of enforcing good work and behaviour. If the child decides not to turn up for the detention (or indeed, simply forgets to do so), the teacher is forced to chase him or her up. This can mean a single classroom incident turning into a cat and mouse game of epic proportions, until the punishment is finally served, or until the teacher gives up and lets the child get away with not sitting the detention. If this happens, the effectiveness of the sanction that was given in the first place is completely undermined.

- *The individual situation*: Finally, sanctions do need to be very carefully tailored to the specific situation in which you find yourself. What works well at a grammar school in a leafy suburb is unlikely to succeed at a deprived inner city comp. When thinking about the sanctions that you're going to use, or whether it is appropriate to use them at all, you will need to consider the school ethos, the type of students you teach and so on. If you are working with children whose natural defence against adults is to become confrontational, then sanctions may well not work in your classroom at all.

So, as you can see, the use of sanctions is a complex and difficult area of your teaching practice. The advice that follows needs to be tailored to your own individual situation if it is to be effective. The ideas and strategies that I give below focus on three different areas. First, the sanctions that are generally available for use and how and why they might work (and indeed not work). Second, how to go about using sanctions properly, if you do decide they are to be given. And, finally, some tips for avoiding the need to use sanctions in the first place.

What sanctions can I use?

Sanctions do vary from school to school – the types that you'll have available to use, the way that they're enforced, and the reaction that the children have to them. Much will be dictated by the school's behaviour policy (if there is one) and the way that this is run. Generally speaking, though, there are a number of commonly used sanctions that you have in your teaching armoury, and these are discussed below. When considering the punishments that you're going to instigate with your class, you will need to think about how effective each type is with your particular students, and again I give some thoughts on this. The sanctions are listed in the order of how 'heavy' each punishment is, from the gentle to the very harsh.

- *The sharp word, look or gesture*: There is a tendency to believe that a sanction has to be the giving of a specific punishment, such as a detention. However, often the most effective sanction will be simply a sharp word or a deadly look from the teacher. Believe it or not, the majority of our students do actually want to please their teachers. Because of this, giving a quick word, look or gesture that shows your displeasure can be surprisingly effective. For instance, you might click your fingers and then point at a child who is just starting to misbehave. This could be enough to remind the student that you are watching for any messing around and that you have noted what he or she is doing. When perfecting your range of 'looks' with the class, do also consider how effective an expression of surprise can be. The unspoken message is that you are amazed that the child would even consider doing such a thing. A look of surprise, rather than one of anger, also takes the heat out of a situation and helps you avoid confrontations. In terms of effectiveness, non-verbal signals such as the word, look or gesture described above can be extremely useful to the teacher. In many cases they will help you avoid the need to give any further sanctions at all. The only drawback is that you have to keep permanently on your toes, intervening with a non-verbal signal as soon as you spot any poor behaviour and nipping it in the bud.

- *The verbal or written warning*: Many behaviour policies now use a verbal or written warning as the starting point for a series of subsequent sanctions. A child's misbehaviour is acknowledged with a quick word or the noting down of a name. The teacher should make it perfectly clear to the student that this is the first step in an escalating scale of sanctions and that, if he or she wishes to avoid going up on the scale, appropriate behaviour must be shown in the future. The verbal warning might involve a quick word in the child's ear, the written warning could be you writing a note in a 'sanctions book', or listing the names of any miscreants on the board. (Although see the points I make in 'Be private' and 'Sometimes be public' below if you do choose to write names up in a public way.)

- *The detention*: There are a number of different types of detention available to the teacher – from a short five or ten minutes (often immediately after the lesson if this occurs before a break, lunch-time or home time) to the longer half an hour or hour long detentions for more serious or repeated offences. Detentions can be an extremely effective punishment, so long as they are something that your children wish to avoid. As I've already mentioned, it is also absolutely essential that you ensure any detentions you set are actually served. Unfortunately, this can make them a very time-consuming method of punishment in a school where the students decide to try it on by not turning up.

- *The phone call or letter home*: Contact with the home is actually a wonderful tool in managing your children's work and behaviour. In many cases the parents or guardians will be only too willing to assist the teacher, but often they are uncertain about how to do this. Many parents are also completely unaware of how their children actually behave at school and a quick phone call from the teacher, advising them about poor behaviour or work, will be welcomed in the majority of situations. When you talk to the parents on the phone, or contact them by letter, do discuss the ways in which you would like them to help support your work in the classroom. For instance, you might set some targets that you would like the child to achieve. The parents can then talk about these targets with their children, at home, and you can make follow up calls to let them know whether or not the targets are being met. The only drawback with school–home contacts is the time and energy involved, but in my experience the improvement in your students' behaviour means it is well worth the teacher putting in the effort.

- *The 'red card' or other final sanction*: The majority of schools do now offer their teachers a 'final' sanction which can be used when a child or a situation has become completely out of control. Having a final sanction as a fall-back position is welcomed by teachers, particularly those who are dealing with potentially violent and aggressive students. For this method to work effectively, the support of senior managers is absolutely essential. They must not only turn up to remove the child from the classroom (if this is how your system works), but they must also be seen to follow up properly on serious incidents every time they occur. In addition, teachers must not be seen to have 'failed' if they are forced to use a final sanction. When you are applying this particular punishment, do be very careful never to threaten it if you are not willing to go through with actually applying it.

See 'Don't threaten what you can't deliver', later in this chapter, for some more thoughts about why this is so important.

How to use sanctions properly

The advice that follows will help you in the use of sanctions in your own classroom. Do bear in mind that the answer is not always in the correct use of sanctions, although this will certainly help, but it may also lie in not using punishments at all, or in minimizing their use. See the section that follows, 'Avoiding the use of sanctions' for some ideas on how you might achieve this.

- *Be clear.* When using sanctions, your very first step must be to make the situation entirely clear, so that there is no room for misunderstandings, and no point in your students complaining that you are being unfair. This means that, right from the word go, the children must know exactly where they stand in relation to sanctions and the way that they are used. Also, when you do have to apply sanctions, this should be done carefully and with clarity. Here are some tips about achieving a clear approach to sanctions in your classroom:
  - *Explain the boundaries*: Let your class know what is and isn't allowed and do this right at the start of your time with the students. Set a series of boundaries (or rules), so that the children know exactly what is expected of them. In most cases the school will already have a set of classroom rules that you can utilize. This explaining of boundaries might be done at the start of the year for a permanent class teacher, or at the start of a day or lesson for a supply teacher. Unless the children know what they are and are not allowed to do, your use of sanctions will inevitably be viewed as unclear and unfair, and problems will arise.
  - *Explain the consequences of breaking the rules*: As well as setting out your boundaries, you should also inform the class of what will happen if they do choose to step outside the rules you have set. If the sanctions are crystal clear right from the start, the children will know what they can and cannot do and there should be no accusations of unfairness.

- *Explain how the sanctions will work*: In addition to letting your class know what will happen if they step outside the limits, you should also make it clear to them how the sanctions will actually be applied. For instance, will you be starting with a low-level punishment, and only gradually increasing this to a more serious one, if the poor work or behaviour continues? Talk to them, as well, about how and when sanctions such as detentions will be served. Tell them too what you will do if they fail to serve the sanction you have given.

- *Be clear when you are having to sanction*: When the time comes for actually handing out sanctions, the clarity described above becomes even more important. If a child misbehaves, or chooses not to work as well as you wish, then take time to make it clear how and why they are going to be punished. Again, this will help you prevent any hint of injustice and it will also assist you in avoiding confrontations.

- *Be consistent*: Consistency in the use of sanctions is, as I said above, absolutely crucial in making them work. However, it is, of course, easier said than done. When you are about to give a punishment, especially to one of your 'worst' children, consider whether you would be giving exactly the same treatment to one of your better students, or whether you would be more lenient on a normally well behaved child. The same applies in reverse: it is tempting to avoid punishing those children who normally work and behave perfectly, but this will be viewed as unfair, or, worse still, you will be seen as a teacher who has 'favourites'.

- *Be fair*: Do ensure that the punishment always fits the crime. When you're in a bad mood, or when a class of children are behaving particularly badly, it's easy to give in to the urge to threaten excessive quantities of detentions at the very first signs of trouble. As we saw above, the children will have been informed about a rising scale of sanctions and it's best if you can stick to this as much as possible, starting at the lowest end of the scale, and only gradually going up if it's really necessary. The fairer you can be with the use of sanctions, the better your children will respond to them.

- *Be private*: If you sanction a child in front of the whole class, don't be surprised if you get a negative reaction. After all, how would you respond if someone punished you in front of an audience of your peers? When you do have to give a sanction, try to keep it on an individual basis, rather than giving in to the temptation to shout across the class. Go over and crouch down beside the child, or ask the student to come to the side of the room for a chat. This strategy has the added benefit of giving the teacher time to calm down and consequently is likely to lead to you dealing with the problem in a more rational and considered way.

- *Sometimes be public*: There will, however, be occasions when you are giving sanctions that you do wish to make a point to the whole class. The key is knowing both when this is appropriate and when it is actually going to work. For instance, if a group of children are messing around and their behaviour is in danger of spreading to the rest of the students, there is no harm at all in having a sharp word with them in front of the class. You should also try to be aware of which individuals are going to react with confrontation to a public dressing down, and consequently try to avoid doing this as far as possible.

- *Be realistic*: When considering whether to use sanctions, and how harsh to be, please don't be too much of a perfectionist. Never lose sight of the fact that your children are only human. Sometimes kids play up because they're bored, or simply because they're having a bad day. Perhaps the work that you're asking them to do is not engaging their interest, or is too easy or too hard? Maybe it's the mood that they're in (for instance on a rainy Friday afternoon) that is causing the problems? Being realistic about just how hard you have to be, and when sanctions are the best route to take, will help you avoid unnecessary stress.

- *But be tough enough*: On the other hand, having said that you need to be realistic, it is also important to be tough enough when you are deciding whether or not to use sanctions. If you are forever giving in to your children and letting them get away with poor behaviour, they will quickly come to believe that it's ok to mess around. You will also be presenting them with a lack of certainty about what is and isn't allowed. In fact, finding a balance between realism and consistency is probably one of the hardest aspects of being a teacher.

- *Be unemotional*: This tactic is very useful if you are working with students who become confrontational when they are sanctioned. Instead of giving the sanction as a punishment from you, explain to the class that you are simply following orders from above. Blame the school policy, explaining that you don't want to give the punishment, but the school insists that you do. When you do this, try to use a tone of voice that suggests how regretful you are about having to use sanctions. This will help you achieve the unemotional approach that is the real key to avoiding incidents of aggression in the classroom.

- *Be human*: Often, it is worth offering a way out of the punishment, or a chance to at least lessen the severity of the sanction you've given. The idea is to make it seem that you're really very generous and that you don't actually want to give sanctions, but that the children are forcing you to do so. For instance, you might set a ten-minute detention, then give the child a chance to 'win-back' five minutes off the punishment by good behaviour for the rest of the lesson. By offering the chance to bargain in this way, you will give the sense that you are a fair and reasonable teacher. Again, you will need to find a balance between sometimes letting children win-back against their sanctions, whilst still maintaining consistency in the way that you punish them.

- *Don't threaten what you can't deliver*: I'm all too guilty of losing my temper with a child or a class, and shouting out '*Right, you lot have got detention with me after school every day for the next week.'* Of course, I have no intention of actually delivering that particular punishment and, as soon as the words are out of my mouth, I regret having said them. Never threaten a punishment that you can't deliver, as it undermines your integrity and diminishes the respect that your children have for you. It also confuses the issue – when does Miss/Sir actually mean what she or he says, and when is it merely an empty threat? In addition, threatening punishments in this way shows you losing your cool, and the students will quickly come to realize that they can get you wound up by misbehaving.

- *Avoid whole class punishments*: When giving sanctions, I would recommend, as far as possible, that you avoid using whole class punishments. I am all too aware that sometimes there is simply nothing else that will work. However, in essence, whole class sanctions are unfair, as it is never everyone who is misbehaving at any one time. Because of this, a whole class punishment will, by its nature, punish at least some innocent children. View whole class sanctions as a last resort and always try to offer a way out of the punishment to the class (see 'Be human' above).

- *Don't talk to them*: Generally, teachers have a tendency to give sanctions verbally, but this can actually be avoided and it could actually be to your advantage to do so. Aim to give at least some sanctions without talking and this will help lessen the overall sense of confrontation your students feel. It will also help you save your voice for more important things, such as teaching. When giving a non-verbal sanction, you might write up on the board: *'If you don't all stop talking and listen to me, you'll force me to start handing out sanctions.'* By the time you've finished writing that, I assure you that your children will be ready to listen! Alternatively, you might simply have a system whereby you write a child's name down the first time they misbehave, then put a series of ticks by the name if the inappropriate behaviour is repeated. The more ticks a child is given, the higher the level of sanction they will receive at the end of the lesson. (Again, you can offer to rub out ticks in return for good behaviour as part of the bargaining process.)

- *Make them worthwhile*: If you do have to give out detentions, then use these in the most effective way that you can. I have found that taking the time to talk with a child about his or her behaviour and why it is inappropriate, can lead to a much better understanding between us in the future. I would guard against always giving work as a punishment (it sends a message that work is something to be avoided, rather than enjoyed). However, if a child has not completed an activity properly during the lesson time, then you are perfectly justified in asking him or her to use detention time to redo or complete it. If your students see that the sanctions you give are going to be used for a positive purpose, they will hopefully feel far less resentful about serving them.

- *Make the punishment fit the crime*: It is also very worthwhile tailoring your sanctions to the 'crime' that the child has committed. For instance, you might give a community sanction, such as picking up litter, to a child who has thrown paper around during the lesson. If a student has drawn graffiti on a classroom wall, then a suitable punishment could be for him or her to scrub all the desks clean. Again, fitting the punishment to the crime in this way gives your sanctions a much more positive and assertive message.

- *Chase them up every time*: When you do use sanctions, particularly detentions, it is absolutely essential that you make sure that these are served. If this means chasing and chasing for weeks on end, then that is what you must do. Unfortunately, if you don't ensure that every single sanction that you give is served, you lessen the impact of the punishments you do hand out. Every time a child gets away with not serving the sanction you have given, next time you do have to discipline the student, he or she will feel that the threat of punishment is an empty one and, consequently, is unlikely to view it as a valid threat.

- *Develop a partnership with parents*: In my experience, one of the most effective sanctions consists of a phone call home to have a chat with parents or guardians who are willing to support you. The idea is for the child to understand that there is a partnership between you and his or her guardians, and that you are quite happy to keep them fully informed about work and behaviour. Although it is a time-consuming sanction, you could well find that a single phone call home works wonders. In addition, you can use the threat of a further contact as a means of keeping tabs on the problem child in the future.

Avoiding the use of sanctions

In some situations, sanctions simply don't work. It might be because of the particular school you are working in, or the specific children that you teach. For instance, your students might be the type who are always getting into trouble, both inside and outside school, and who are all too used to being punished. Consequently, they could become very defensive or even aggressive when you do try to use sanctions. In addition, excessive use of sanctions does tend to lead to a negative atmosphere in the classroom. As a professional, you will be developing your teaching skills much more fully if you do try to find ways of avoiding the need to give sanctions. Here are some ideas about how you might do this.

- *Focus on rewards*: The use of rewards is always preferable to the use of sanctions, although it can be all too easy to forget about them when you're coping with poorly behaved children. Rewards create a positive atmosphere in the classroom and they suggest a teacher who is in control of his or her teaching. Rewards will help you maintain good relationships with your children and they will also tend to be much more successful in gaining good behaviour. When considering the use of rewards, make sure that you use those ones which your students really want to earn. There is no point at all in giving out merit marks if the children do not respond well to this reward. In my experience, I've found that children tend to be best motivated by a concrete, material reward, something tangible. For instance, you might give a chocolate bar to the child who shows the best concentration, or offer a sticker for every ten minutes of hard work that a student does. Try to tailor the rewards to the individual – some children love to earn merits, while others will be far better motivated by the offer of a phone call home.

- *Change the subject*: When faced with poor work or behaviour, before you wade in and start handing out sanctions, consider whether you can make a quick intervention, change the subject and avoid having to give a punishment at all. For instance, you notice that Brian is annoying the boy who sits next to him, by scribbling on his work. Instead of immediately handing out a sanction to Brian for the misbehaviour, try instead calling him over to your desk and asking him to hand out some materials for you. By changing the subject in this way, you will distract Brian from the misbehaviour, which is probably only attention seeking in the first place. If you can give him your attention without acknowledging the inappropriate behaviour, then he is far more likely to avoid it in the future.

- *Use humour*: I firmly believe that we underestimate the effectiveness of the use of humour in the classroom. Teachers who can respond to silliness or even poor work or behaviour in a humorous way, rather than immediately feeling the need to give out sanctions, will generally develop a much better relationship with their children. They will also avoid unnecessary confrontations. For instance, if a child simply will not be quiet and listen when you are talking, try running over to the student, getting down on your knees, and begging melodramatically for a bit of peace and quiet. The class will be amused at seeing you do this and it should surprise the child into shutting up.

- *Have a sanctions amnesty*: If you work in what is euphemis-tically known as a 'challenging' school, or with what we might term 'difficult' students, then it could be worth reconsidering whether it is sensible to use sanctions at all. In these types of situations, punishments generally lead to more and more serious confrontations within the classroom. If this is the case for you, why not try going for a week or longer, without resorting to detentions or any other type of punishment? This will force you into finding other ways of keeping order and getting hard work, and you may well find that you come up with some ingenious ideas along the way. You might decide to explain to the class your plan not to use sanctions, or you could keep your decision private from them.

10 The class of widely varying abilities

Q. *The class that I teach contains children with a huge range of different ability levels. I have some children who basically cannot read or write, and others who are at least a year or two ahead of their actual age in these skills. I feel like some of my students are being held back in their learning, while there are others who are all at sea with the work that I ask them to do. I'm running myself ragged trying to get around to help all my children and I just don't feel that I'm doing any of them justice. I do attempt to differentiate the tasks I set, but it's proving almost impossible without me working 24 hours a day, every day of the week. Do you have any tips on how I can set work that's suitable for all the children in my class?*

A. Working with a class of widely differing abilities is a real test of the teacher's skills. Stretching the most able, while still catering for those with learning difficulties, is a complex and difficult task. If we are to do the best for all our students, we do of course need to ensure that the work we set matches their ability levels. In addition, unless the teacher can keep the children interested and motivated in the work that is set, behaviour issues will inevitably arise. In an ideal universe, teachers would work with small numbers of children and be given plenty of time to plan appropriate activities, taking the needs of every individual into account. Unfortunately, in the real world, it simply is not possible for us to differentiate every single activity for every different child that we teach. There are, however, some strategies that you can use to help you with this difficult situation. Try some of the tips and ideas below to help you with differentiation in your own classroom.

- *Use group projects*: Although project work has fallen out of favour somewhat, it does in fact offer a very useful way of differentiating for classes of widely varying abilities. When the teacher sets a task that allows for teamwork within the group, the children will naturally differentiate by their own input. For instance, a child who has good leadership and administrative skills might take on the role of organizing the group, allocating tasks to the appropriate individuals. Another child who is brilliant at art might take responsibility for the artistic and creative aspects of the work and so on.

- *Use your 'experts'*: As well as having different ability levels generally, children also display talents or expertise in various areas of the curriculum. For instance, you might have a child with very poor literacy skills, who speaks three different languages. Similarly, you might teach a student who finds maths very difficult, but who is an artistic genius. When this is the case, the sensible teacher will utilize the expertise of his or her class in the teaching as a whole. For instance, you could ask the trilingual child to teach his or her classmates some words in another language, or the artistic student to teach the class about perspective. Sharing their skills and talents with the class in this way will be very motivational for the children, it will develop their confidence and speaking and listening skills. It will also help their classmates to learn about new areas, perhaps ones about which you yourself have no knowledge. In addition, it will, of course, give you as a teacher a bit of a break from the teaching!

- *Develop a bank of worksheets*: Part of my armoury as a teacher includes large numbers of worksheets that I have developed over the years to cater for varying abilities within my classes. As you go through your career as a teacher, make sure you keep copies of any worksheets that you create, especially where these apply to children of different ability levels. Ask around too for copies of worksheets that other teachers have produced – in my experience your colleagues will be only too happy to help you out by giving you a copy of their own work.

- *Adapt your worksheets*: When making a computerized work-sheet, it is a fairly simple task to create three or four different types, aimed at varying levels of ability. For instance, you might offer your more able students more complex vocabulary, simplifying the terms and words you use for those who struggle with literacy. For less able children, it is also useful to put any instructions in a box, making these as clear and simple as possible and to use a bigger typeface, so that the writing is easier to read.

- *Think about extension-tasks*: Often, our brightest children will finish the work we set more quickly than their classmates. If this is the case in your classroom, then take some time to think about activities that these high ability children can do once they've finished the main work you have set. I have found that my very clever students really enjoy memory tasks, such as learning a poem or a set of difficult spellings off by heart. Another activity that you can set is for them to do background research on a topic to be shared with the rest of the class at a later date.

- *Stretch the most able and the least*: It is tempting for us to actually underestimate what our children are really capable of achieving. We might stick to the curriculum require-ments as they are laid out, when in fact our children could respond to being given work at a much higher level. This applies to *all* children and not just the most able. For example, I was only taught about pathetic fallacy, the term for the weather mirroring events in literature, when I took my A level English course. However, I have taught this term to children in Year 7 and they responded very well to my offering them what they saw as 'advanced' work. Even though the less able might not have fully understood what I was teaching them, they were able to access the idea at its simplest level. The same applied when I taught French to a reception age class – they loved the idea and all the children were able to join in! I also discovered that I had an 'expert' in the class – a girl who could speak French fluently and who was delighted to be asked to help me out with my pronunciation. This approach is also very popular with parents, who like to see teachers stretching their children, and who will be very pleased that you are doing so.

- *Give vocabulary lists*: Where you have a wide range of abilities in a class, vocabulary lists can be very helpful. You could type up a list of 50 technical words connected to the subject being taught, starting with the most simple and moving on to the really advanced. When you give out the list, you can challenge the children both to learn the spellings and also to find out the meanings of the words. The higher ability students could be asked to start halfway down the list, while the less able might concentrate on the initial, more simple words. This would also make an excellent homework activity in a whole range of curriculum subjects.

- *Pair them up*: Although mixed ability teaching has fallen out of favour somewhat, an effective method of helping both the least and the most able children is to pair them up to work with each other. By approaching classroom tasks in this way, both parties will learn from their peers. For instance, the high ability students might learn how to explain a task simply and clearly to a less able child. These pairings could take place throughout a lesson, but the technique might also be used for an able child who has finished the work and who needs something to do for the remainder of the lesson.

- *Get all the help you can*: It is always worth making the most of any help that is on offer, whether this is a classroom assistant in the primary school, or perhaps a parent or sixth former at secondary level. These helpers could be asked to work on an extension-task with the most able, or on simplified activities with the least able. Never be afraid to ask for, and accept, help in your classroom. Many hands make much lighter work for the stressed teacher!

11 The child who does no work

Q. There's one child in my class who never seems to produce any work. I have to keep on his back all the time, nagging on and on at him to complete the activities I've set. At the end of the lesson, he might have done a couple of lines of writing, but this is usually completely illegible. I've tried giving him a sanction, such as a detention, for the lack of work, but this just doesn't seem to help. Now the other children are commenting on how he 'gets away with' not doing any work, and some of them are starting to try it on with me as well. What can I do to improve the situation?

A. As teachers, our key job is, of course, to teach and when a child is apparently not making any progress it is very frustrating. We all want to do our best for the students, but sometimes an individual will provide a real challenge for you when it comes to completing the work that you set. You start to feel that you are letting the student down and, perhaps, you worry about what the child's parents or guardians might think. With the added pressure for our classes to do well in statutory tests, the situation begins to cause a great deal of stress for the teacher.

With the child who simply refuses to produce any work, or who will only complete the minimum and that to a very low standard, the initial focus must be on discovering exactly what the problem is. I've given some ideas how you might do this below. Once you have established the root cause of the lack of work, you can then set about solving the problem, using some or all of the strategies that I describe.

- *Find out what the problem is*: It might sound obvious, but when dealing with a child who doesn't produce any work, the first move you should make is to identify exactly what

the problem is. There are a number of factors that might be at work:
- a learning difficulty;
- lack of understanding of the lesson content;
- being easily distracted;
- lack of motivation;
- disaffection with school or with the subject being taught;
- laziness.

- *Make an SEN assessment*: The next step with any child who has difficulty in producing a reasonable quantity of work is to get the student assessed to check whether he or she has any special educational needs. The difficulty may be specific to a particular curriculum area – perhaps the child is dyslexic or has motor skill issues that mean he or she cannot hold and use a pen properly. Even if the problem is not with a particular skill area, it could be that there is an issue with concentration or behaviour and, again, this could be because of a special need. Approach the appropriate special needs staff at your school to ensure that any problems are picked up on and dealt with at the earliest possible stage in the child's education.

- *Give an individual explanation of the tasks*: Sometimes, the child will simply not understand what you have asked him or her to do. It could be that the student finds it difficult to listen to you when you give a whole class explanation of the tasks, or it could simply be that this particular child is less able than the others in the group. It will really help if you can find time to sit down with the individual, preferably near the start of the lesson, and go through exactly what is required. While you are doing this, use the target setting strategy given below to set the student an objective to aim for in completing the work.

- *Move the child*: If the issue is with a child being easily distracted, consider whether it is the proximity of another student that is causing the problem. Some children find it easy to work and chat simultaneously, while others can only concentrate on a single activity at any one time. If this is the case in your situation, a quick and easy solution is to simply move the child to sit on their own, or next to a very quiet and well-behaved student. Alternatively, insist that the whole class works in silence for a period of time.

- *Set targets*: When a child finds it impossible to do more than the tiniest amount of work, the setting of targets can be especially useful in solving the problem. At first, you might set a fairly straightforward target, for instance completing only a very small piece of work, so that the student has something specific but easy to aim for. You could then increase the complexity of the target gradually over time, as the child begins to meet the standards you set. For a child who gets distracted easily, targets can be a very useful approach because you can refer to them every time you feel the student is going off-task. There are various different types of target that you might use:
  - *Visual targets*: For the child who lacks concentration it is particularly helpful for the teacher to put visual targets on the page, as these give the child something very specific to focus on. For instance you might draw a line halfway down the page and ask the student to aim to write down to this line by the end of the lesson.
  - *Number targets*: Another method of setting targets is to give a specific number for which the student must aim. This might be writing a particular number of words, or answering a specific amount of questions. Children seem to really enjoy meeting these types of number targets, so it is well worth giving this approach a try.
  - *Time targets*: An alternative option is to tell the child that you want a certain amount of work done within a set period of time, perhaps combining this with the two suggestions above. This might result in you asking for five questions to be done in ten minutes, or for the child to write down to the line you have drawn within half an hour. Another idea is to tell the student that you will return to check on his or her work in a certain number of minutes, or at a specific point in the lesson.

- *Use rewards*: Hand in hand with the targets described above goes the use of rewards when the student does achieve a certain target. Rewards are an excellent way of motivating the easily distracted or the disaffected student. Although it is time consuming, it is a good idea to set a short target and respond to its completion with an instant reward. This tends to work better than expecting the child with poor concentration or motivation to respond to a more general, longer range target. Aim to use rewards that the child values very highly, whether this is stickers, merit marks, a 'time out' from work, or whatever best suits the individual. The keener the student is to receive the reward, the more likely he or she is to achieve the target you have set.

- *Make the child feel special*: We all want to feel that we are special in some way, and using this fact can be a very helpful approach in motivating a child who seems to be disaffected by school. It really is worth turning the focus away from the work for a while and trying, instead, to develop a sense in the child that he or she is important and unique. This should hopefully pay dividends in the child's whole approach to your lessons. There are a wide range of approaches you might use to make your problem student feel special. Here are just a few ideas:
  - Give the child an important task to complete, such as tidying up your stock cupboard or watering the class plants.
  - Let the child feel like an adult, for instance by asking him or her to be teacher for a while and explain a part of the lesson to the class.
  - Find out where the child's talents lie, for instance break dancing or skateboarding, and ask the student to demonstrate some moves to the class.
  - Greet the child by name at the beginning of the lesson and say how much you are looking forward to working together.
  - Keep returning to the student during the lesson, checking up on how well he or she is working, setting targets and giving rewards, and always using the child's name to ensure continued motivation.

- *Find the key to motivating the child*: For every student, there will be a key to unlocking the natural motivation that school can beat out of us. It is the teacher's job to find this key, especially when a child seems to lack this essential motivation in his or her work. In the past I have used activities related to football teams to motivate some of my disaffected students, or worked on creating slang and rap versions of literary texts for those kids who just don't see the point in school. It should be possible for you to adapt any curriculum area to engage even the most poorly motivated child.

- *Make the work topical*: Along with finding the key to motivating children, making the work you set topical will engage even the most disaffected student. Crazes come and go, so look for the latest toy or pop group and find some way of incorporating this into your lessons. It might be that you write a story from the viewpoint of Buzz Lightyear, or that you set a group task in which the children set up their own Pop Star competition.

- *Use 'props'*: When looking for ways to motivate individual students and classes as a whole, I find that bringing objects into the classroom from the world outside of school can be incredibly effective. Children seem to be fascinated by seeing an object that wouldn't normally be found in a classroom. For instance, you might bring in a carved wooden box and ask the children to write about what is inside. Alternatively, you could buy some exotic fruits and ask the students to discuss the countries that they come from, offering them the reward of tasting the fruits if they do good work.

- *Unlock the imagination*: School can be very boring, and in many subjects it might seem impossible to add that creative touch that makes the work fun and leads to increased motivation. If you are struggling to get your children to produce their work, it is well worth adding a touch of imaginative spice to the learning so that they are re-enthused about school, even if this means deviating from the statutory curriculum for a while. In Science, you could bring in a magic wand and let the children create potions to cast spells on each other and on you. In History you might set up the classroom as though it were a specific time from the past, and then get the children to play characters living in that age.

- *Let them be children*: Along similar lines to the idea above, do let your students be children from time to time. What I mean is, to release the 'big kid' who lives inside each one of us. I have found that this strategy works across the board, even with students who are right at the top end of secondary school. For example, everyone loves the chance to make a mess, so you might do some finger painting or build sand castles.

- *Go in hard*: Finally, an alternative approach is to take an entirely different tack and to go in really hard on the child in question. Explain the sanctions that you are going to use for a lack of work and instigate them as necessary, following right through to the 'ultimate' sanction if required. This method is likely to be most effective where the issue is simply one of laziness, rather than one of a learning difficulty, or an issue with motivation. Make it clear what you expect to be completed by the end of the lesson and explain the sanction that will arise if the child does not achieve the goal you have set. How well this will work depends on the exact situation in which you find yourself and you will need to use your professional judgement to decide whether it is going to work for you.

12 The over emotional teacher

Q. *I sometimes wonder if I'm just too emotional to be a teacher. When a child is difficult, for instance swearing at me or refusing to follow an instruction, I feel my eyes start to well up with tears. Sometimes I have to leave the room before I burst out crying. I also find myself getting wound up really easily when my kids muck around. My heart starts pumping and my temper begins to rise, and then I lose my rag and start shouting at them. Now I'm starting to question my ability as a teacher – maybe my children mess around like this because I'm useless at my job? Perhaps I should just quit and go and do something else? Please can you give me some advice about how to keep my emotions under control?*

A. The vast majority of people who become teachers do so because they genuinely care about children, and want to help them succeed. Many teachers will develop a strong bond with their children and their class or classes over the course of the academic year. Naturally then, when a child throws your care back in your face, or stops you from offering the high quality learning experience you want to give the class, you are bound to get emotionally involved. As a teacher, finding ways to deal with your inner emotional reactions is all part of learning to behave and respond as a professional. It is not easy at first to bottle up your natural responses to misbehaviour, but it really is essential that you find ways of doing this if you are to work as a teacher for the long term. Otherwise, like the teacher in the question, you may find yourself questioning your own abilities and considering leaving your job to do something easier and less emotionally draining.

There are a number of problems with an emotional reaction such as that described in the question, especially if this is to incidents of misbehaviour. First, if the children see you getting upset and/or angry, then you are giving them an incentive to misbehave again in the future. '*Let's see if we can get Miss/Sir to cry again*', is a very good reason for repeating poor behaviour, especially when a large proportion of the class are involved in messing around. Second, an emotional reaction is very draining for the teacher – not only in terms of its impact on you as a person, but also because you may feel guilty about what you view as a loss of control. Reacting emotionally is also problematic because it means that you will not be able to deal with the situation rationally and you could find yourself becoming overly defensive or negative with your children. Over time, if you find that you cannot handle day-to-day classroom issues without bursting into tears, or losing your temper, then you are unlikely to want to stay in the teaching profession. The suggestions below give you some pointers about ways to keep your emotions in check.

- *Don't take it too seriously*: Although it's tempting to get completely involved and engrossed with your work when you're a teacher, at the end of the day it is only a job. Try to learn not to take things too seriously and this will help you avoid becoming over-emotional. Refusing to take life seriously will also help you deflect the poor behaviour that can be so demoralizing for us as teachers. For instance, if a child is rude to you, rather than allowing the insult to hit home, try instead simply laughing it off. Laughter has a very beneficial effect on your stress levels and it will also negate any effect that the child might achieve by trying to hurt you.

- *Keep a perspective*: Carrying on from the idea above, do always remember to keep a perspective about your job. If a group of children are messing around and you find yourself getting frustrated and responding emotionally, then take a step back from the situation and view it with a sense of perspective. It really isn't the end of the world if there's a little bit of poor behaviour in your class – children are children, after all, and misbehaviour doesn't always have a completely rational cause. If you can aim to keep a sense of perspective at all times, you will help yourself avoid the need for excessively emotional responses.

- *Put the walls up*: If you are working with difficult children, or in a tough school, then you will need to learn to put a wall between yourself and poor behaviour or negative attitudes. This is essential for the long term, because if you react emotionally to difficult situations, you will eventually become worn out and over stressed. An excellent idea is to build an invisible barrier between yourself and the children who are misbehaving. Allow this metaphorical wall to shield you from feeling hurt and instead let the poor behaviour simply bounce off it.

- *Change your attitude*: I know from my own bitter experience that it is all too easy to see misbehaviour as being aimed at you personally, rather than as something that the children are simply doing of their own accord. You might begin to feel that you are useless as a teacher, that the children are picking up on this and that their poor behaviour is, consequently, a result of your own incompetence. I know I have certainly had this emotional response in the past, when working with difficult classes, and that I have begun to question my own abilities as a teacher. The key for survival is to change your attitude to incidents that occur. Instead of blaming yourself, see the issue as the children's problem, something they are choosing to do because of the way that they are, rather than because of anything you as a teacher have done. If you can adapt your attitude to classroom incidents in this way, you will find it far easier to retain confidence in your teaching abilities and to take a positive and assertive approach with your students.

- *Take your breaks*: I'm well aware that it is all too tempting to work through break times, because of the huge workload that comes with being a teacher. However, if you do find that you have difficulty keeping your emotions in check, you will need to be in tip-top condition when you are in front of the children. It is therefore absolutely essential that you take your breaks: having a bit of time off from the kids will help you work much more effectively when you are in the classroom and assist you in dealing with any difficulties that do arise. Make a real effort to get to the staff room during the day, and when you're in there try not to talk about your children all the time (although this can be a useful way of letting off steam). Sit down with a drink, take a few deep breaths, and then chat with your colleagues about what you watched on TV last night, or some other subject completely unrelated to school.

• *Leave work at work*: I do, of course, appreciate that the majority of teachers do often need to take some work home with them simply to get it all done. However, there will be times when you are feeling particularly tired that you need to stop yourself from doing this. At the end of the day, when you go home, try leaving school behind you completely. Even if this means that you don't finish all your marking, or that your lesson plans are not as detailed as you might wish, the most important thing is your own physical and mental health. Learn to give yourself a break by leaving work at work on occasions.

13 Too tired to teach

Q. *Some days when I get into school I feel completely exhausted, even before I've had to face my children. My life outside of work is demanding – I have family commitments that mean my evenings and weekends are very busy. I'm getting to the stage where I dread coming into work, because I'm just completely shattered, and that's such a shame as I used to really enjoy my job as a teacher. Last week I put my head down on my desk for a few minutes at lunch-time, and fell fast asleep for almost an hour! I feel like I'm not doing my best for my students, because I simply don't have enough energy to teach them properly. What can I do to improve the situation?*

A. Teaching is a very demanding job, not only mentally and emotionally, but also physically. This is perhaps especially so if you work with the very youngest end of the age range, or if you teach an active or practical subject such as PE or Music. It can also be the case that you will get tired if you teach students whose behaviour is putting a great deal of pressure on your classroom management skills. Dealing with difficult children all day is bound to put a strain on you. When you're completely exhausted you will be doing no-one any favours – your children's education will suffer, and your own health may come under threat. It's therefore vital that you do find some strategies for keeping the tiredness at bay.

The tips that I give below offer you a range of different ways to stop yourself getting so tired in the first place and of coping with tiredness when it does arise. If you do want to stay in teaching in the long term, you will need to cut yourself a bit of slack from time to time, so please don't see my suggestions as laziness, but rather as ways of retaining your sanity and keeping yourself healthy. It is only if we can learn to find a bit of balance in our working lives, that we will be able to do the best that we possibly can for our students.

- *Give yourself some lessons off*: There is absolutely no harm at all in taking some lessons off when it is necessary. What this means is that you should find some ways of giving your children lessons that are easy for you, ones that allow you to sit back a bit and get some rest. Here are just a few suggestions:
  - *The computer room*: Put your children in front of computers, set them a task to complete and you will generally find that they are more than happy to just get on with it. Many of our students are, in fact, far more competent at computer use than we, their teachers, so take advantage of this fact when you need a lesson off.
  - *Private reading*: Primary teachers, and secondary teachers of English, can easily justify a half hour or an hour of silent reading from their classes. This is incredibly restful for the teacher, especially if you do it last thing in the afternoon, or on a Friday, when the children are relatively docile. Being able to read for extended periods, in silent concentration, is also, of course, an important skill for them to learn.
  - *TV or video*: Watching an educational video or television programme with your class, preferably one that lasts for more than a single lesson, is the perfect way of giving yourself a rest. Before you get started, do take the time to check that the equipment works properly, as this will save you the stress of having a disorganized opening to the lesson.
  - *The test*: Giving a test, in which the children must work in complete silence, is very restful for the exhausted teacher. From time to time it really is worth the extra marking load that results from setting an examined piece of work, just to have the chance to give yourself a lesson off. While the children are sitting the test, plonk yourself down at your desk and relax.

- *Balance your teaching day and week*: It really is not possible to make every single lesson a full-on, energetic and enthusiastic presentation by the teacher. If you find yourself getting extremely tired, think carefully about the balance of each teaching day and also of your week as a whole. Are there particular times of the day or week when your energy levels dip and how might you adapt the type of lessons you teach to take this into account? Is there a specific class or subject area that needs some high quality (and energy-heavy) input, and another that you can sit back from for a little while? Take a look at your overall timetable for the week and balance out your input to give yourself the chance to overcome tiredness.

- *Decide what's really important*: In teaching, there will always be too many demands on your time. It can become very tiring if you try to do too much, especially if you are taking on commitments outside the classroom. Prioritizing your workload and deciding what really is and is not important, is vital in keeping you fresh and enthusiastic about your work. Most of the time, you should put your classroom teaching at the top of the list, way ahead of doing admin and other non-essential tasks. Learn to say 'no' when people ask you to attend a meeting, or to run a club after school, if you're too tired to do so. On the other hand, it could be that you will actually feel less tired if you spend some time on extra-curricular activities, as this might help to re-enthuse you about your work. You will need to look carefully at your own situation to help you make this decision.

- *Consider your teaching style*: Some teaching styles are much more wearing than others, so if you do find yourself completely exhausted, take some time to consider whether your style in the classroom is contributing to this. The 'strict and scary' approach that I describe in my book *Getting the Buggers to Behave* can be very effective, but it is also extremely hard work for the teacher to sustain. Alternatively, if you are not being firm enough with your class, this could be leading to poor behaviour, which is in itself very tiring for the teacher. If this is the case for you, there are lots of tips in this book about how to deal with misbehaviour in the classroom, particularly in the chapter entitled 'The class from hell'.

- *Check the noise levels*: Excessive amounts of noise in the classroom can be tiring for both the teacher and the children and can also lead to an escalation in behaviour issues. In addition, if the teacher always has to shout to be heard, this will become exhausting over a period of time. If your classroom is a very noisy place, or if you do find yourself having to shout frequently, try to find some ways of keeping the volume levels down. You will find a whole section devoted to the issue of effective use of your voice on p. 135 ('The worn-out voice'). Here are just a few ideas about how you could keep the noise levels in check:
    - *Use non-verbal signals*: As much as possible, learn to find ways of communicating with your children without using words. To do this, you could set up some key signals to which your children will respond fairly instantly. For instance, a hand on the head might mean that you want silence and everyone sitting down in their seats; a downturned palm could indicate that you want the children to calm themselves.
    - *Use your body, not your voice*: In addition to teaching your class some non-verbal commands, learn to use your body language rather than your voice to get the class to do what you want. For instance, standing with arms folded and simply waiting for silence can be an effective method of gaining attention with many classes. Think about the ways in which you can communicate using body language and try to replace the use of your voice as far as possible, so that you retain your vocal energy for your teaching.
    - *Keep the volume down*: When you do have to talk to your children, make sure that you do this using as low a volume as you can. This will help keep the noise levels down, as well as forcing the students to learn to listen more carefully to you when you talk. When you are dealing with misbehaviour, this is one of the times that you need to be most aware of how loud you are talking. A

quiet approach is not only good for you as a teacher, but it will also tend to help you solve behaviour issues more easily, because it lessens any sense of confrontation.

- *Balance noisy times with silence*: Although we obviously do need to have times when the class is making a lot of noise, learn to balance these with silent activities. You can even offer this as a reward to your children – '*I'm going to let you do this noisy activity, but afterwards we're going to work in silence for fifteen minutes*'. In the partnership that should exist between teacher and children, it is important that the students are taught to respect your wishes and to understand when silence is necessary.

- *You be teacher*: An excellent technique for the tired teacher is to hand over the reins for a time by allowing one or more of the students to 'be teacher' for a while. Children love being given this opportunity and it also allows you to take a rest. You might ask one of your very able students to teach a topic of his or her choice to the rest of the class. You could give instructions to a child about what you want the activity to involve and he or she can then relay these to the class. I've also found that children absolutely love being asked to write up instructions or ideas on the board. This can be used as a reward for good work or behaviour and, at the same time, give you a short break during the lesson.

- *Be ultra strict*: Poor behaviour is extremely wearing over time, especially those low-level incidents such as chatting, going off-task and so on. If you are feeling the strain, then it is worth being ultra strict with your students (always provided that they will respond to this, rather than simply deciding to take you on). If you are working at secondary level, you will normally find that you are able to take an ultra strict approach with Year 7 students, for instance insisting that they work in silence for a few lessons to give your poor thumping head a rest. At primary level the children are generally more malleable and you should be able to instigate an 'ultra strict' approach without too much trouble.

- *Minimize your workload*: If you are feeling very tired, for instance towards the end of the term, then do find ways to 'cheat' and minimize your workload. This applies particularly to marking, and other paper-based tasks, which take up so much of our time. For instance, you might spend a series of lessons doing oral activities, so that there is no marking to be done. Alternatively, you might get the children to mark their own exercise books once in a while, asking a student to call out the correct answers while you take a break.

- *Have a bit of fun*: Sometimes, tiredness can be caused when the fun has gone out of our work and the job seems like a daily grind, rather than the exciting career we had envisaged. If this is the case with you, then find some ways to have a bit of fun with your children. Whether it's playing *The Weakest Link* with your class, or doing some really messy painting activities, having a bit of fun with your children will remind you about why you came into the job in the first place.

- *Get out and about*: Moving on from the point above, if you do need to put the fun back into your work, then why not get out of the classroom for a while? Being outside of our usual environment is always refreshing and it can inject that vital bit of enthusiasm back into our lives. You could throw that boring lesson plan out of the window and head out on a nature trail. You might get involved in setting up an exciting trip or take your class into the hall for a bit of improvised drama.

- *Get some helpers involved*: Teaching can be quite a lonely job at times and when you're feeling tired you might find yourself feeling very isolated. In fact, though, there are plenty of people out there who you could get into your classroom to lend a hand and also to take some of the strain out of your working day. Why not ask for parents to volunteer to do an activity with your children – perhaps you might find someone who is an expert on a particular area of the curriculum, such as a scientist or a writer. Think too about other agencies from outside the school that you could involve, such as the police or health workers.

- *Use your holidays wisely*: The temptation is always there to use our holidays to catch up on all that work that remains undone. I know that I have driven home at the start of many breaks with a pile of books to mark in the back of my car. However, if you are suffering from exhaustion, you would be wise to use your holidays for the best reason – to take a break from work and give yourself a rest. If you can afford it, why not fly away somewhere sunny, leaving all your school work behind? Alternatively, take some time out from work concerns and spend some quality time with your family or friends.

- *Call in sick*: If the worst comes to the worst, there is always the option of taking a day or more off sick. You might not view tiredness as meaning you are ill, but exhaustion, combined with stress, can in fact become a medical issue. If you are really feeling the strain, go and visit your GP and ask to be signed off for a few days. You will serve the children much better on your return.

14 The worn out voice

Q. I'm in my first year of teaching and am forever getting sore throats and infections. Sometimes, by the end of the day, I can hardly speak, let alone teach my children. I feel ok on a Monday morning, but by Friday my voice is all raw and used up. If I can't sort this problem out, I don't see how I'm going to continue being a teacher in the long term. Do you have any tips that might help me?

A. For us as teachers, our voices are the primary method we have of communicating with our students. Whether we are monitoring behaviour, setting a lesson, praising an individual child, or any one of a myriad of other daily tasks, we all need to talk almost every minute of our working lives. The voice is the teacher's instrument, but unlike a violin player, the teacher cannot simply replace his or her instrument if it gets worn out. It is absolutely vital, therefore, that we learn how to use our voices properly early on in our careers. We also need to find ways of limiting our use of verbal communication. You can find a whole range of ideas about how you might do this in the sections below.

   As well as it being crucial to take care of your voice, many of the techniques and ideas discussed below also make for good classroom management approaches. For instance, the teacher who uses interesting tone and modulation in his or her voice will tend to engage the children's attention more fully and conse-quently receive better work from them. The teacher who avoids shouting at all costs will be seen by the children as being in control of his or her emotions and is likely to get much better behaviour from the class. I've split the tips and strategies for helping with this problem into two sections: the first deals with taking care of your voice, the second with ways of limiting the amount of speaking you actually do.

Taking care of your voice

- *Control the volume*: If you listen when you are walking around a school, you will often find that the voices of teachers are audible from the corridor. This fact alone suggests that we do tend to use excessive volume levels, especially as there really is no need to speak particularly loudly to be heard by our students. Most classrooms have reasonable acoustics, which means your voice will carry fairly easily (although I do acknowledge there are some teaching spaces that can cause teachers real problems with voice projection). Remember, the quieter you are, the more attentive your children will need to be to hear you, so try at all times to control the volume of your voice and keep it as low as possible. Use the approach described below to train yourself into doing this.

- *Learn to 'hear' yourself*: When you're teaching, from time to time take a moment to mentally step back and listen to yourself. Ask yourself: how loud am I speaking and is it really necessary to speak this loudly to make myself heard? I like to use the picture of the volume control on a stereo to help explain this approach – try turning the sound of your voice down, for instance from a level 7 to a level 4, or even a level 2. Your children will soon tell you if they can't hear you and if they do complain, then my first suggestion would be that they must learn to listen more carefully!

- *Never, ever shout*: A teacher who shouts, particularly one who does so on a regular basis, is bound to be damaging his or her voice. Shouting also gives a very specific message to your children, whether this is that you are a strict and authoritarian teacher or, more probably, that you are unable to control your temper when you are faced with misbehaviour. Shouting not only suggests a loss of self-control, but it is also a rather rude way of interacting with people. You would be unlikely to shout at your colleagues if you worked in an office, so take a similar approach within the school environment. My firm advice to you would be that, as far as possible, it is best to never, ever shout at your students. Try to catch yourself in the seconds before you open your mouth to bellow and use the quiet but deadly approach instead (see below).

- *Be quiet but deadly*: Carrying on from the point above, it is generally far more effective to be very quiet but very deadly sounding with your children, when you do need to discipline them. A quiet tone of voice demonstrates a high level of control – it shows how confident you are that your instructions will be followed and it also shows that you are entirely in control of your own emotions and responses. Using the quiet but deadly approach is also an excellent way of preventing the class from being an audience when you do need to enforce discipline with an individual. It is far better to get up close to the child to discuss his or her behaviour, rather than screaming your thoughts across the class.

- *Control the tone*: Sounding quiet but deadly, as described above, is about controlling the tone of your voice. Being able to do this is all part of being an effective teacher. There are various tones of voice that will prove useful in addition to the quiet but deadly approach. For instance, you could use a very happy, excited tone to create a positive atmosphere and indicate how much you are looking forward to working with the children. You might try a very sad and unhappy tone if the children are not doing as you wish. It can also be helpful to adopt a tone of surprise and disappointment if an individual does misbehave. This tone is in fact far preferable to an angry one, which only tends to encourage confrontations to develop.

- *Control the speed*: Think too about using a range of different speeds in the way that you speak. Enthusiasm and a sense of pace and energy can be created by a fast, excited voice. You can also use a slow, almost hypnotic speed when you need to calm a class down or prepare them for some quiet and very focused work. Again, learn to hear yourself when you talk, speeding up or slowing down your voice as appropriate.

- *Get their attention first*: It is particularly common for teachers to speak too loudly when they want to address the class and need to get the children's attention. In a noisy classroom, you may find yourself calling out for the class to be silent so that you can address them. However, shouting for attention is rarely, if ever, necessary. There are plenty of other ways in which you can get your children to be silent and ready to listen. You can find lots of ideas below about how you might do this. Look too at the points I make in the chapter on 'The talkative class'.

- *Have a calm and quiet classroom*: Teachers who talk quietly and who are able to create a calm and controlled atmosphere in their classrooms, will obviously tend to put less stress on their voices. If noise and exuberance is a particular issue with your classes, then do think about how you might create a more restful atmosphere with your children. Here are a few ideas and points to note:
  - *Group work tends to be noisy*: By their very nature, group activities do tend to create a noisy and excitable atmosphere in the classroom. Consider using individual work for a while to limit the noise levels of your children. When you do need to use group work, make it clear that any discussion must be done in relative quiet.
  - *Noise breeds noise*: Following on from the point above, you will certainly find that the noisier your classroom is to start with, the louder it will get over time. It is inevitable that this will happen, because as the volume levels get higher, the children will need to speak more loudly to be heard. The situation can escalate very quickly if the teacher does not keep constantly on top of the amount of noise that is being made.
  - *Use your voice to calm them down*: As we saw above, a quiet voice, with good tone and modulation, can be a very effective tool. I have found that it is possible to use my voice to create a calm and slow feeling with my children, for instance when describing how they should approach a task. A droning, almost hypnotic tone of voice will quickly calm even the most lively and talkative children.

- *Use a silent rule*: There is no harm at all in insisting that your students work in complete silence at times. In fact, in my experience some of the best work is done when the class is completely quiet, because all the children are able to concentrate properly. If you feel that this suggestion is excessively hard on the students, you can always give them 'time-outs' every twenty minutes or so for a quick chat.
- *Create a calm atmosphere*: Consider the use of different resources for creating a feeling of calm in your room. For instance, you might play a soft and quiet piece of music to quieten your children at the start of the day. Alternatively, you could lower the lights (if this is possible) to bring down the general levels of excitement and noise.
- *Look at the environment as a whole*: Do think, too, about how the general environment might be affecting your children's mood and approach. Some colours are more calming than others, for instance pale blue is a very relaxing colour. Think also about how crowded or hot your room becomes and the effect that this has on the overall mood and atmosphere.
- *Use focus exercises*: These are exercises that create a calm, almost meditative atmosphere for your children. A well-focused child will find it much easier to concentrate on the work that you set and will also be less likely to talk too loudly. You can find some examples of focus exercises in the chapter on 'The little fidgets' on p. 65.

- *You be teacher*: I find this technique very helpful, not only for saving my voice from over-use, but also because the children really enjoy it and consequently it makes a very useful reward. Choose a student to act as 'teacher', either for a brief period or for a longer stretch of time. This student then takes over teaching the class, while you get a well-deserved rest! You can sit beside the child to prompt him or her in the instructions that need to be given, but you will not need to raise your voice to address the class.

- *Use student-led activities*: If you find that your voice is suffering from over-use, it is important to consider some ways in which you might make less actual use of your voice. This can be done by using student-led, rather than teacher focused, activities. For instance, set a series of tasks to be completed in a small group and this will put the emphasis on the children speaking and listening to each other, rather than to you. Ask your class to prepare 'show and tell' work, where they work in pairs or groups to develop and then present their ideas to the class. You can then sit with the groups to listen in on their discussions, perhaps assessing their speaking and listening skills at the same time.

- *Drink plenty of water*: I have found over the years that my throat does tend to dry out when I'm teaching, particularly when I'm giving a lesson that requires a lot of talking. Consequently it's very important to have a bottle of water (or other drink) close to hand at all times. Take frequent sips of water during your teaching day, especially when you are doing 'chalk and talk' type work (i.e. teacher-led work from the front of the class). Many teachers forget, or are unable, to take their breaks and they therefore miss the opportunity to have a drink. Keep a bottle of water with you at all times to ensure that you don't get dehydrated.

- *Get some voice training*: If possible, try to access some INSET work on using your voice properly. If you can find a course run by a professional voice coach (someone who normally works with actors), this will prove invaluable in helping you keep the strain out of your voice. A good voice coach will be able to teach you much more about how we actually use, and abuse, our voices.

Limiting verbal communication

- *Use non-verbal communication*: Of course, as teachers we need to communicate with our students pretty much all day, every day. The temptation is to focus on doing this by using your voice, but in fact non-verbal communication is, in many ways, a far more effective teaching tool. Communicating without words shows a teacher fully in control of his or her classroom; it also allows you to give very private hints to individual students about what they are doing right or wrong. Non-verbal communication can take a huge range of different forms. Here are just some ideas about how you might communicate with your students without using any words:

- *Your eyes*: The most effective teachers are able to indicate their inner state simply by the look in their eyes. This might be an expression of anger, puzzlement, surprise, praise, disappointment and so on. Try staring in silence at a child who is talking to a friend when they should be listening to you. You will quickly find that the child becomes aware of your gaze, turns to see you staring and (hopefully) falls silent in embarrassment.

- *Your face*: In my experience, an arched eyebrow, a deadly looking stare, or a furrowed brow can be a hugely effective signal that I am not happy with a child's behaviour, and that it should stop now. In fact, these very tiny, subtle signals should and can be enough to silence a whole class, and gain their attention. The teacher with an expressive face will be able to keep his or her verbal communication to an absolute minimum.

- *Your hands*: Similarly, hand signals can be very useful in classroom management. You might click your fingers to indicate to an individual whose attention has wandered that you have noticed what is happening; you could hold both hands out, palms down, to indicate that you want the class to calm themselves; you might prop your chin on your fist to indicate how bored you are in waiting for the students to fall silent.

- *Your body*: Body language really is a hugely effective tool for the teacher who wishes to put across his or her feelings in a non-verbal way. Standing with your arms folded, combined with a raised eyebrow, indicates that you are waiting for the class (and that you are not particularly happy about having to do so!). Placing your hands on your hips demonstrates an assertive attitude without the need to open your mouth.

- *The space*: The way in which the teacher moves within the space can also give the class a great many different non-verbal signals. For instance, if you move to stand close to a child (without opening your mouth), this gives the clear message that you want something from that individual. The child will, more than likely, be aware of what he or she is doing wrong. You can simply stand there, looking mean, until the inappropriate behaviour stops.

- *The power of doing nothing*: One of the most powerful non-verbal signals in the classroom is, paradoxically, when the teacher does absolutely nothing at all. Our children are used to us fighting to get their attention, and working hard to teach them as much as we can and, consequently, when we suddenly become still and silent this sends a very powerful message. It does take a lot of courage (at first) to stand completely still, refusing to talk until the class falls silent and gives you their attention. However, if you can master this signal and get your class to understand what it means, you will save yourself a huge amount of verbal interactions.

- *The power of gesture*: While teaching drama, I have done a very successful scheme of work on the use of sign language. As well as teaching the sign alphabet (which the children love learning), I have also spent a series of lessons working on how people who speak different languages might find ways of communicating with each other. This scheme looks particularly at the use of gesture, and I have found that all my students respond really well to a teacher who uses gestures (not necessarily pre-agreed with the class) to indicate what he or she wants. For instance, the classic finger to the lips for silence, or the slightly more powerful 'zip your mouths up' gesture to indicate that the class should be silent. Similarly, there are a huge range of gestures that indicate when you want your children to sit down and be silent. In my experience, the more humorous the gestures, the more effective they are. For instance, I might try gesturing that my head is about to explode because of the high level of noise, or pretending to sob desperately or bang my head on a desk because I simply cannot cope with a class any longer.

- *Use signs and signals*: In many ways, working with large groups of children is like working with dogs: proper training is crucial if you wish to develop good behaviour. This can be fairly easily done by the use of specific signals to indicate your wishes, combined with rewards for obeying these signals. Early on in your time with a class, it is very useful to spend time defining a number of different signs and signals that you are going to use to indicate exactly what you want the children to do. These signs will allow you to avoid unnecessary use of your voice when communicating your wishes to the class. If you bring these signs into play from the start, you can train your students in the correct behaviour, and in fact they will probably enjoy the whole process. Remember to reward the children for the correct responses, for instance using praise, time-outs, or whatever works best with your particular class. Here are some examples of signals to which you might train your children to respond:

- *The 'sit' signal*: Just as we might train a dog to sit at a specific signal, so we can train our children to sit (and fall silent) by using a gesture of some type. This 'sit' signal is particularly useful if you are working with young children, for instance in a reception class, or if you are a teacher of a practical subject such as PE, Music or Drama. You may have groups working noisily on a variety of different activities and the sit signal allows you to draw the class together and get them sitting back as a group, without the need for verbal interactions. Your sit signal might be simply the teacher going to sit in his or her chair; it could be holding both hands in the air; it might be a single blast on a whistle. Train your children to respond as quickly as possible without the need for you to say anything. When they are quick to observe the sit signal, praise them lavishly for their observational powers. If they are too slow, set a challenge for next time, or spend some of the lesson practising until they are responding as quickly as you wish.

- *The 'attention' signal*: Similarly, it is very useful to have a signal of some type for gaining your children's attention. One technique I have used very successfully, particularly with small children, is to click or clap my hands in a specific pattern (for instance, 2 slow then 3 quick clicks). The children are trained to join in with the pattern, which the teacher then slows down gradually until the class falls silent. The children find it pretty much impossible to continue talking when they are having to concentrate on clicking their fingers.

- *The 'time left' signal*: There will be many times when you want to re-focus your class on the activity at hand, for instance if they are getting a little noisy while doing their work, or if some of them seem to be going off-task. Letting the students know how much time is left for the work will also give them a target to work towards. When you have your children's attention, you might gesture to your watch, and then hold up five fingers to indicate that there are five minutes left. You can then repeat the signal as the time gets progressively less and less.

- *Use written instructions*: Although we do often focus on giving verbal directions to our children when we are setting work, in many ways written instructions are actually more useful. If a child is working from the board or a worksheet, he or she can refer back to the text to see what the next activity should be, rather than having to remember the teacher's verbal instructions given earlier in the lesson. If your children are not yet old enough to follow written instructions, then why not try using symbols or pictures instead?

- *Have periods of complete silence*: Depending on your individual style as a teacher, you may feel that it is not necessary for children to work in complete silence, or you may believe that this is how all classrooms should be. If you are struggling with a worn-out voice, insisting that your class do work in total silence is in fact a very useful technique. Once you have them working in this way, if you do need to talk to them at all, they are already silent and you will not need to raise your voice. Complete silence is also very restful in the classroom and this will help the children to concentrate fully on their work. It will also keep you calm so that the tendency is for you to talk more quietly and, consequently, put less strain on your voice.

15 School on my mind

Q. How on earth do I stop myself from thinking about school all the time? It gets to the end of the day and I find that I just can't switch off my mind from worrying about work – why this child is misbehaving, why that child isn't achieving better results, what lessons I still need to plan for next week and on and on. I get home and find my brain still buzzing – there are a million things that I have to remember to do and they just spin round and round in my head, when I should be relaxing in the evening. I spend every weekend thinking about school, to the extent that I'm dreaming about it on a Sunday night. I feel really nervous about going back to work at the start of each week and I don't understand why.

A. Most teachers will admit to the fact that school preys on their minds, particularly towards the end of a holiday period. This is never more true than at the end of the summer holidays, when you go back to work after a long period away from the classroom. Even those staff with years of teaching experience will find themselves worrying, or at least thinking, about school at this time of the year. When you first start out in teaching, it can seem like these worries are taking over your life. You may find the concerns reoccurring whenever you have a break from school, for instance after a half term or holiday break, or even after each weekend, as for the teacher in the question above.

Finding a way to make a divide between your professional and your home life is vital if you wish to stay in the teaching profession for the long term. Unless you can achieve this balance, you will quickly find yourself becoming overloaded, stressed out, and generally worn down by the demands of your work. The first step towards resolving the issue for yourself is to decide exactly why school is preying on your mind so heavily. Once you have sorted this out, you can start to put into place some strategies for overcoming the problem. Why, then, do we have a tendency to think about school all the time, even when we are not actually at work? Consider the different ideas below and which apply particularly to your own situation.

- *Fear of the unknown*: At the start of the year, much of the worry comes down to the fact that your children are an unknown quantity. You might have to face a whole new class in a primary school, or you could be working with a large number of students you have never met before in a secondary school. As well as the stress of worrying about behaviour and other classroom management issues, you also have the huge pressure of learning a whole set of new names and getting to know a group of new people.

- *Fear of the known*: On the other hand, the worries that you have might arise from actually knowing what to expect when you do arrive at school. For instance, if you have to face the proverbial class from hell on a Monday, you are of course going to be thinking about this on a Sunday (and probably contemplating whether or not you feel sick enough to stay off school). Worries about poor discipline are high on most teachers' lists of concerns and the knowledge that you have to control and teach a very difficult group of students can, understandably, prey heavily on your mind.

- *Fear of 'forgetting' how to teach*: After a period away from the classroom, it can feel rather worryingly as though you might have 'forgotten' how to teach. I know that I have had this fear regularly when facing a class after some time away from school. Of course, teaching is actually like riding a bicycle – once you've learnt how to do it, you never really forget. But the fear that you might have is often enough to make a return to the classroom a real concern.

- *Inexperience*: If you're new to the job, it could be that worrying about school all the time is a result of inexperience. When we first start out in teaching it is inevitable that we are making mistakes on a more or less daily basis, and this can be demoralizing and highly stressful. You might feel that you are simply not up to the job, perhaps fearing that you might fail your induction year. Hopefully, once you have a few more years' experience under your belt as a teacher, the weekly or termly nerves will start to disappear.

- *A sense of vocation*: Teaching is, for most of us, a vocation as well as a job. There is a tendency for teachers to get fully involved with their work and with their children, so that it becomes an integral part of their lives. If you do have a child in your class whose home life is very difficult, it is almost unavoidable that you are going to care deeply about what happens to that student. Consequently, it becomes difficult to switch off your emotional attachments to your work when you get home.

- *The demands of the job*: Carrying on from the point above, teaching does make huge demands on us as individuals. We invest vast amounts of emotional, psychological and physical energy in our work and it is, perhaps, inevitable that it might begin to take over our lives if we allow it to. As well as the demands of the classroom, we also have the added pressure of the non-teaching parts of the job, such as administration and meetings. All in all, it is hardly surprising that we tend to think about school when we are not there.

- *Unpredictability*: Doing a job in which you deal with people is, by its very nature, unpredictable. It can be hard to know how individual students are going to react to you from one day to the next. It is also difficult to predict how the class as a whole will behave and respond. Sometimes a child will become abusive or confrontational, perhaps for no good reason, and this is very hard to cope with. You must also learn to deal with the unpredictability of situations where you have to manage very challenging behaviour, such as violence or aggression.

- *Excessive workload*: Of course, the problem of having school constantly on your mind may come about simply because you have far too much to do! If your workload is excessive, it is inevitable that you will be thinking and worrying about all the tasks that you must get completed. Perhaps you have recently been promoted to a managerial post and you are finding it difficult to cope with the added pressures, and to regain the work/life balance you had achieved as a classroom teacher. A new promotion will almost inevitably lead to a teacher with school weighing heavily on his or her mind, at least for a while.

- *Missing something vital*: When we do have a very heavy workload, some of the tasks that we 'must do' are going to have to slip a little. The worry that you might forget to do something that is absolutely vital, especially if you have a number of critically important tasks to complete, can create a sense of dread in the over-worked teacher.

So, if you do find yourself in a situation where school is constantly on your mind, what exactly can you do about it? One of the most important things is achieving that difficult balance between being a perfectionist and allowing yourself to relax if you do get things wrong. This balance is very hard to achieve and it may take you a number of terms, or even years, to do it. Here are some tips and strategies that you might like to try in your attempts to keep school off your mind.

- *Don't take your work home with you*: Although it is incredibly tempting to take work home, especially when you have far too much to get done, you do need to give yourself a break from your work. If you don't manage to achieve a work/ home balance, you will be doing no-one any favours, least of all the children you are trying to teach. Be as strict as you can with yourself – I would recommend staying in school to work until 6.00pm or so, then simply leaving behind what cannot be completed. You may well find that you complete much more work at school than at home, as you are keen to get it finished and get out of there. By literally leaving your work at school you will help yourself create a psychological break between your workplace and your home environment. Of course, I do appreciate that this may not be possible for those teachers with commitments at home. If this is the case for you, why not set yourself a couple of hours in the evening to devote to work, and stick to this time limit religiously?

- *Refuse to take on too much*: To help you in your quest to have at least some time for your own life outside of school, do get into the habit of refusing to take on too much. For instance, commit yourself to one extra curricular activity by all means (it's actually very good for helping you relax), but refuse to also attend a series of meetings that will eat into your after school time.

- *Keep a notebook of things to do*: You may find that you are at home and a thought pops into your head about something you should have done/must do at school. When this happens, the tendency is to dwell on the task and to allow it to worry you, especially if it is one of those vital jobs mentioned in the section above. Instead of thinking about school outside of the working day, it is worth keeping a small notebook in which you can add to your lists of things to do. You can then check this at school in the morning and decide what you really must do, and what can be put off to another day. To help you prioritize, you might have two (or more) lists: one for tasks that are absolutely vital, another for those that can wait if necessary. A third list might detail those jobs that you would love 'to do' if you only had the time.

- *Learn to prioritize*: As I've said before, it really isn't possible in teaching to do everything that needs doing. The key, therefore, is to learn to prioritize. Look at the range of jobs that need doing and decide which ones must be done, which ones you would enjoy doing and which ones you could conveniently forget about. Once you've done this, chuck any guilty feelings out of the window and concentrate on those really important areas of your work.

- *Learn to delegate*: Whenever you do come across a task that doesn't have to be done by you personally, then learn to delegate it to somebody else. Your children will be more than willing to take a large number of classroom jobs off your hands. Get them involved in putting up displays, helping to mark each other's work, presenting parts of the lesson, and so on. If possible, delegate some of your administrative workload to other staff within the school. For instance, instead of typing that letter yourself, ask in the office to see whether someone will do it for you.

- *Take up a hobby*: If you do find your job occupying your every waking thought, then it really is a good idea to find yourself some interests outside of school. Try to choose a hobby that will occupy your body or mind completely and allow you to wipe the children out of your mind for a while. School tends to make demands on our minds over those it places on our bodies. Physical activities are therefore very useful for clearing the brain and for tiring your body out as well as your mind. A repetitive exercise such as swimming can be meditative and help you relax; a sport that requires focus, such as rock climbing, will aid you in putting school behind you at the end of a hard day. Other less physical activities that might prove useful are those that require deep concentration, such as hobbies involving arts or crafts.

- *Don't approach school with expectations*: Often, we will dread a particular class or a specific student, and the worry will build up way beyond what is actually realistic. The knowledge that we must face this class or this child hangs over us so that we start to actually fear coming into work. Although I know it's hard, do try to avoid having expectations about how a class or a child will behave in advance of the actual experience. If you do expect the worst, invariably your fears will be realized. If, on the other hand, you approach the situation with a positive and light-hearted manner, you will at least be in the best position to cope with any problems that do arise.

16 The paperwork issue

Q. *I just can't seem to get on top of my paperwork. There is always a mountain of marking waiting to be done on my desk, and my 'to do' pile is enormous. I'm sure there are papers at the bottom that I should have dealt with weeks or even months ago, but I just don't seem to have a moment to get around to them. Now report writing time is coming up and I know that the pressure is going to get even worse. Last time I had to write reports, I was up until midnight for three days in a row getting them finished and my teaching suffered as a result. My pigeonhole looks like a bomb has hit it, but I just can't face looking at even more bits of paper. I'm getting really fed up of taking paperwork home with me – if I have to do this much admin, rather than enjoying my work in the classroom, then maybe I should give up on being a teacher and go and do something else?*

A. Paperwork really is the bane of many teachers' lives, perhaps all teachers' lives. The main problem and annoyance is that it gets in the way of the really important parts of our jobs. The feeling that you are behind with your paperwork can cause a great deal of stress for teachers and it is all too tempting to bury your head in the sand and just ignore that huge bundle of papers in your pigeonhole. However, when report writing time comes around, or when some vital marking has to be done, there is simply no way to avoid getting to grips with the administrative side of the job.

Of course, the way that we deal with our paperwork is very much down to the individual teacher. Some people are incredibly well organized, they have every piece of paper filed or dealt with as soon as it arrives on their desks. With other teachers, you know better than to put that important memo in their pigeonhole, because it will just sit there for the next month or so before slipping out and onto the floor, to be lost forever! Hopefully you should be able to adapt the tips below to suit your own personal style of dealing with paperwork, and to help you lessen your own administrative workload.

Before looking at some strategies for actually dealing with the paperwork, let's take a brief look at the different bits of paper you might have to deal with in the course of your work as an ordinary classroom teacher. (Please note that the list does not include all those managerial tasks that have to be completed if you are in a promoted post.) By studying the different parts of your administrative workload in this way, you will find it easier to follow the tips given in the following section, for instance on prioritizing your workload. Looking at the long list that follows demonstrates perfectly exactly how heavy the average teacher's administrative burden is!

- Teaching:
  - lesson plans – writing, organizing, filing;
  - schemes of work – writing, developing, changing to fit new syllabus;
  - worksheets and other teaching resources – writing, creating, adapting.

- Assessment:
  - marking class work;
  - marking homework;
  - marking exams;
  - marking coursework;
  - report writing;
  - assessing special needs.

- Form filling (on a huge range of subjects):
  - completing government forms;
  - filling out SEN forms;
  - completing forms for your school.

- Professional development:
  - applications for INSET courses;
  - feedback on INSET courses;
  - self-evaluations.

- Pastoral:
  - reports on your form group;
  - absence letters – chasing up, filing;
  - letters to parents on a range of subjects;
  - other form group related paperwork – filing;
  - creating certificates.

- Extra-curricular:
  - memos about activities;
  - trips related paperwork, e.g. risk assessments;
  - forms for insurance;
  - letters home about trips or other activities;
  - forms for booking travel arrangements.

Let's take a look now at some of the different strategies you could use in order to keep your paperwork under control. As you gain in teaching experience, I promise that you will find it easier to be more ruthless in your dealings with paperwork and other administrative tasks.

- *Find a balance*: Although I've said it before, I really am happy to repeat myself: teaching is all about finding a balance that works for you and your children, and that allows you to do the best possible job, without driving yourself into a nervous breakdown. When dealing with the administrative aspects of your work, you must decide exactly how much time the paperwork in question deserves, and whether the time would be better spent in some other way. There are only a limited number of hours in a day, and if you wear yourself out with paperwork you will not be able to give your children the highest quality learning experience.

- *Learn how to prioritize*: At the end of the day, there is simply no way that you can deal fully with every bit of paper that you receive. Clearly, some of your paperwork will be very important, some of it far less so. There will be some bits of paperwork that you must deal with immediately, others that you need to hold onto for information and some that can go straight in the bin. If it's not essential that you deal with or keep a piece of paper, then brace yourself and chuck it on the recycling pile.

- *Clear your pigeonhole each day*: I have always found it useful to clear out my pigeonhole on a daily basis, if at all possible. That way, you avoid the build-up of papers that can lead to a feeling that there is far too much to deal with and a consequent burying of your head in the sand. In addition, if you do receive an urgent piece of paperwork, as does sometimes happen, you will be able to deal with it on the spot. You will also appear very efficient to the other teachers at your school.

- *Bin it*: Be as strict as you can with yourself about whether or not to keep the pieces of paper you receive. If in any doubt at all, it is best to chuck them straight in the (recycling) bin. Inevitably, someone else will have a copy of any really essential pieces of paperwork and you can always take a photocopy if it does prove to be necessary. In my experience, schools do tend to produce far more paper than is actually needed and the bin is probably the best place for many of the bits of paper that are issued by your school.

- *Deal with it*: If a piece of paper can be dealt with immediately, then doing so will ensure that your paperwork stays to a minimum. For instance, if you are given an SEN form to fill out on one of your students, try to complete it immediately, rather than agonizing over what you are going to put. It is probably going to be far more useful for the SEN staff to receive a brief, but quick response, than to wait for ages for a more detailed and considered reply.

- *Pass it on*: The great thing about passing on the bits of paper you receive is that they are no longer your problem. You might need to deal with them in some way first (see above), but as soon as you have done this they can go straight into somebody else's pigeonhole. Whenever possible, pass your paperwork on to someone else straight away.

- *Filing and the teacher*: In my experience, teachers do have a tendency to hoard and file far more paperwork than is strictly necessary. Be ruthless about what you file – only keep what you will definitely use again. Most of your filing should be connected to your lesson planning, as inevitably you will reuse resources and lessons over the years. Be ruthless, too, about weeding out your files, perhaps once a year when you have a quiet period at school. Much of the paperwork you have will quickly go out-of-date too. For instance there is no point in keeping an exam syllabus unless it is applicable to the current year, so chuck any old paperwork away.

- *Use empty time for paperwork*: Quite a lot of time spent in schools is empty or wasted time that can be utilized for administrative tasks. For instance, during a staff briefing you might listen out with one ear for any announcements that particularly affect you, while doing some quick marking or form filling at the same time.

- *Don't take paperwork home with you*: I would strongly advise that you get into the habit of staying on at school after work to deal with paperwork tasks as far as is humanly possible. There are a couple of very good reasons for this. First, the urge to be finished and to get home tends to lead to less time being spent on the paperwork than might be the case if you took it home with you. Second, if you do start to take your paperwork home, the habit will quickly escalate and you will find your home life being overtaken by your school life, with piles of books or papers cluttering up your home. And of course this is not at all conducive to relaxation.

- *Operate a 'clear desk' policy*: Psychologically, it is very helpful to have a clear desk policy. Instead of coming in for the day and having to look at a huge pile of papers scattered over the surface, a clear desk puts you in a positive frame of mind. Of course, it is best to have a clear desk because you have actually dealt with every single piece of paper, but even if your clear desk policy means simply piling all the bits of paper into one or two piles, this will again help you to feel less overwhelmed by admin.

- *Beware of the 'to do' mountain*: Like all teachers, I have a habit of creating a 'to do' mountain when it comes to paperwork and administrative tasks. There are so many things that I mean to get done, if only I can find the time and, consequently, I hang onto far too many bits of paper. If I were brutally honest with myself, I could quickly dump at least half of these, in the sure and certain knowledge that I will never have sufficient time to actually deal with them. In teaching there is always something 'to do'. Be as strict as you possibly can with yourself about which administrative tasks must take priority.

- *Good enough is good enough*: I read this tip recently in the *Times Educational Supplement*, and felt it was a very worthwhile summary of a sensible position on admin. If you work as a teacher, there will never be enough hours in the day to be a perfectionist at your job. Make do with 'good enough' rather than beating yourself up that things could be done better.

- *Make time for vital paperwork*: In the question, the teacher mentions the pressure of having to write reports. Report writing time is always very stressful, because the task comes on top of all the other aspects of your work. If you know that reports are coming up shortly, there are a number of useful approaches you can take to minimize the stress:
  - *Get started early*: Do start writing your reports as early as possible, especially if you have a large number to complete. It might be that you can make a start on reports right from the earliest part of the school year, making brief notes on what you are going to say about your students as you go along.
  - *Plan some 'easy' lessons*: Don't stress yourself with any heavy duty teaching when you are under the pressure of report writing. If possible, set some lessons in which you can spend half an hour working on your reports, for instance setting the class a silent reading task.

- *Hold back on the marking*: When it's report writing time, try not to set class work that requires a lot of marking. For instance, you might do some oral assessments or a long-term project with your students to keep your marking workload to a minimum.
- *Use time-saving techniques*: Find any methods that you can to save yourself time, and don't feel guilty about using them. You might write three standard reports on a computer, for poor, average and good students, and then adapt these to suit the individuals in your class. You might write your reports using extra large handwriting, or ensure that your signature takes up a good part of the page.